2 Writing
for the Real World

STUDENT BOOK

AN INTRODUCTION TO BUSINESS WRITING

Roger Barnard | Antoinette Meehan

OXFORD
UNIVERSITY PRESS

Contents

1 Introducing yourself

> **IN THIS UNIT YOU WILL LEARN HOW TO ...**
> ▶ write an introductory email to a business acquaintance
> ▶ check your knowledge of email format
> ▶ write a short description of your job and career

1 An email to a customer

1 Read the email quickly. Why is John writing?

To:	Rita Singh
Cc:	
Subject:	Introduction

Dear Ms. Singh,

This is a short email to introduce myself. My name is John Weng, and I replaced Tony Lee as Tokyo branch manager of Axis Sportswear at the beginning of this month. I joined the company five years ago, and previously I was assistant manager of the Singapore branch office.

RS Imports is one of our most valued customers, and I look forward to doing business with you in the future. If you have any queries, please do not hesitate to contact me.

Sincerely,

John Weng

2 Are these statements true (T) or false (F)? Check (✓) the correct box.

		T	F
a	John is writing to an old friend.	☐	☐
b	He started his new job last month.	☐	☐
c	He started working for Axis five years ago.	☐	☐
d	Rita Singh works for RS Imports.	☐	☐
e	John wants to meet with Ms. Singh very soon.	☐	☐

3 Write the words and phrases in the email that have the same or similar meanings as the ones below.

a brief   _____
b started working for _____
c before that   _____
d clients   _____
e working with   _____
f questions   _____
g feel free to   _____
h get in touch with _____

2 Writing about your work experience

1 Use the information below and the words and phrases on the left in exercise 1.3 to complete the introductory email from Jenny Ho.

name: *Jenny Ho*

she replaced: *Jim Baker*

position: *Marketing Manager*

company: *Viva Cosmetics*

started new job: *September 1*

joined company: *three years ago*

previous position: *sales representative*

To: Vita Delgado

Cc:

Subject: Introduction

Dear Ms. Delgado,

This is a ¹ *brief* email to introduce myself. My name is Jenny Ho, and I ² _____ Jim Baker as ³ _____ manager of Viva ⁴ _____ on ⁵ _____ I. ⁶ I _____ the company ⁷ _____ ago, and ⁸ _____ that I was a ⁹ sales _____ .

GH Enterprises is one of our most valued ¹⁰ _____ and I look forward to ¹¹ _____ with you in the future. If you have any ¹² _____ , please feel ¹³ _____ to get in ¹⁴ _____ with me.

Sincerely,

Jenny Ho

2

To write about your work experience, you can use these forms:

I replaced Tony Lee (as sales manager) I was appointed sales manager		at the beginning of this month. last month. in July. on July 1. two years ago. in 2004.
I	joined	the company the I.T. Department
Before that, Previously,	I was	with Costco Stores. assistant sales manager. in the publicity department.

Complete these sentences by using the correct prepositions or no preposition (−).

a I started work ＿＿＿＿＿ September 21.

b He left Excel Engineering ＿＿＿＿＿ May last year.

c Ms. Garcia joined our department ＿＿＿＿＿ the end of last month.

d She was appointed Vice President ＿＿＿＿＿ last month.

e Oscar Bruni started working for the company ＿＿＿＿＿ 2002.

f I graduated from college ＿＿＿＿＿ three years ago.

▶ See page 129 for more information about times, dates, and prepositions.

3 **Make notes about your work experience. Use real or imaginary information.**

present company / department / job:

started:

previous company / department / job:

4 **Use the notes to write two or three sentences about your work experience for an introductory email.**

3 Email format

1 Number the sections of Rita Singh's reply to John Weng in the correct order, 1–5.

☐ Thank you for your email and congratulations on your new job.
   I look forward to working with you in the future.

☐ Rita Singh

☐ Sincerely,

☐ To: John Weng
   Cc:
   From: Rita Singh

☐ Dear Mr. Weng,

2 Match the email sections from exercise 3.1 above with these headings:

a complimentary close _____   d signature _____
b main body _____   e email header _____
c salutation _____

▶ See page 111 for more information about emails.

4 Writing task 1

Imagine that you have just started your present job (real or imaginary). Write an introductory email to a business acquaintance (real or imaginary). You can use the email in exercise 1.1 as a model and the information you wrote about yourself in exercise 2.4.

5 Writing task 2

Exchange emails with a classmate and write a reply. You can use the email in exercise 3.1 as a model.

6 Writing and you

Ask a classmate the questions below and complete the questionnaire with their answers.

---

1 What kind of business writing do you do in English?

emails ☐
letters ☐
faxes ☐
memos ☐
reports ☐
Other: _____

2 Who do you write to in English?

business acquaintances ☐
customers ☐
colleagues ☐
Other: _____

3 Do you like writing in English?

Yes, very much. ☐
Yes, it's O.K. ☐
No, not very much. ☐
No, I don't. ☐
If you don't like it, what is the reason?

_____

4 What do you find difficult when you write in English?

grammar ☐
vocabulary ☐
punctuation ☐
spelling ☐
format (email, letter, etc.) ☐
levels of formality and informality ☐
Other: _____

5 What would you like to do during this course?

I'd like to work on my …
grammar ☐
vocabulary ☐
punctuation ☐
spelling ☐
Other: _____

2 Arranging meetings

1 Two emails

1 Read the emails.

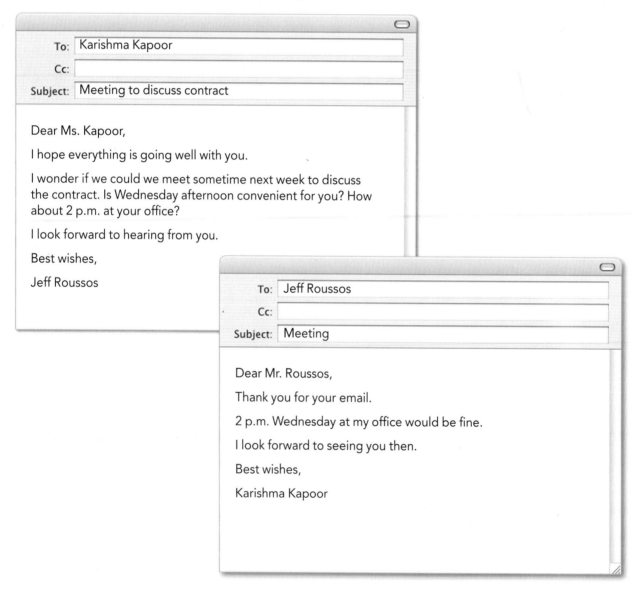

To: Karishma Kapoor

Cc:

Subject: Meeting to discuss contract

Dear Ms. Kapoor,

I hope everything is going well with you.

I wonder if we could we meet sometime next week to discuss the contract. Is Wednesday afternoon convenient for you? How about 2 p.m. at your office?

I look forward to hearing from you.

Best wishes,

Jeff Roussos

To: Jeff Roussos

Cc:

Subject: Meeting

Dear Mr. Roussos,

Thank you for your email.

2 p.m. Wednesday at my office would be fine.

I look forward to seeing you then.

Best wishes,

Karishma Kapoor

2 Answer the questions.

    a When does Mr. Roussos want to meet Ms. Kapoor?

    b Where does he want to meet?

    c Why does he want to meet Ms. Kapoor?

    d Can Ms. Kapoor meet him?

    e Are the emails formal or informal?

2 Suggesting a meeting

1

LANGUAGE FOCUS

To suggest meeting someone, you can write:

I wonder if we could meet sometime next week.

Could we meet sometime next week?

It's a good idea to mention the topic you want to discuss:

I'd like to	discuss	the details of the contract.
	talk about	your estimate for the new offices.

You can combine the sentences above like this:

I wonder if we could meet sometime next week to discuss …

Could we meet sometime next week to talk about … ?

To suggest a time and / or place you can write:

Would Tuesday morning at 10 a.m. at your office be convenient for you?

How about Tuesday morning at your office?

Write two sentences for each situation below. Use different expressions each time. Pay attention to punctuation and capitalization.

a meet later this week / discuss the new company website
Friday / 9:30 a.m. / your office

_____

_____

_____

b meet sometime this month / talk about the staff shortages
Monday November 20th / my office

_____

_____

_____

2 Write two sentences suggesting a meeting, topic, and a time and place. Use your own ideas.

_____

_____

_____

3 Replying to a request for a meeting

LANGUAGE FOCUS

Always respond promptly to a request for a meeting. When you agree to meet, you can confirm the details like this:

2 p.m. Wednesday at my office would be fine (for me).

When you cannot meet, use:

I'm afraid	Friday afternoon isn't possible.	
I'm sorry, but	I have another appointment I'm in a meeting I'm out of town	(on) Friday afternoon.

When you refuse a request, you should usually suggest another time and / or place:

How about Thursday? 11:00 a.m. would be good for me.

Respond to the requests.

a Could we meet next Tuesday at 10 a.m.? (agree)

_____

_____

b I wonder if we could meet tomorrow afternoon. (refuse)

_____

_____

c Could we meet this Friday morning? (refuse)

_____

_____

d I wonder if we could meet sometime this week. (agree)

_____

_____

4 Changing arrangements for a meeting

1 Read the emails quickly and answer the questions.

a Why is Mr. Roussos writing?

b Can Ms. Kapoor meet him on Friday?

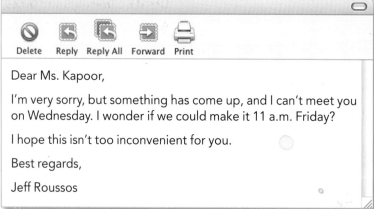

Delete Reply Reply All Forward Print

Dear Ms. Kapoor,

I'm very sorry, but something has come up, and I can't meet you on Wednesday. I wonder if we could make it 11 a.m. Friday?

I hope this isn't too inconvenient for you.

Best regards,

Jeff Roussos

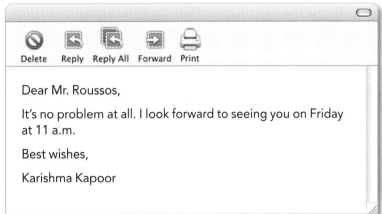

Dear Mr. Roussos,

It's no problem at all. I look forward to seeing you on Friday at 11 a.m.

Best wishes,

Karishma Kapoor

2   LANGUAGE FOCUS

If you can cannot keep an appointment, you can start:

I'm (very) sorry, but I'm afraid	something has come up I have to change my plans for next week,	and	I can't meet you on Thursday. our Thursday meeting isn't possible.

Suggest another time and / or place:

I wonder if we could make it 11 a.m. Friday?
Would 11 a.m. Friday be possible?

End with an apology:

I hope this isn't too inconvenient for you.
I'm very sorry about the inconvenience.

When you respond to a change in plans, you can use:

It's no	problem inconvenience	at all.	I look forward to seeing you on Friday at 11 a.m. 11 a.m. Friday is fine with me.

Rewrite the emails in exercise 4.1 using the alternative phrases above. Use the same days and times.

A _____

  _____

  _____

  _____

B _____

  _____

  _____

  _____

5 Times, dates, and prepositions

Fill in the blanks using *at*, *in*, *on*, or – (no preposition).

1 Maybe we can meet _____ sometime next month.
2 I wonder if we could meet _____ 2 p.m.
3 Are you free _____ Monday?
4 Could we meet _____ the morning?
5 I'm afraid I have another appointment _____ Tuesday afternoon.
6 I'm sorry, but I'm busy _____ all next week.
7 I look forward to meeting you _____ July.
8 I'm afraid I'm out of town _____ the 23rd.

▶ See page 111 for more information about times, dates, and prepositions.
128

6 Formal or informal?

LANGUAGE FOCUS

All the emails in this unit are written in a polite, friendly but quite formal style. If you know a business acquaintance well, you can use a polite, less formal style:

MORE FORMAL	LESS FORMAL
Salutation and closing:	
Dear Ms. Kapoor,	Dear Karishma,
Best wishes,	Best wishes, (or no closing)
Jeff Roussos	Jeff
Pronouns and auxiliary verbs:	
I'm very sorry, but …	Very sorry, but …
I look forward to meeting you next week.	Look forward to meeting you next week.
It's no problem at all.	No problem at all.
Vocabulary and expressions:	
I hope everything is going well with you.	How are things with you?
I wonder if we could meet …	Could we meet …
Is Tuesday convenient?	Is Tuesday OK?
Thank you for your email.	Thanks for your email.
I look forward to seeing you then.	See you then.

Rewrite the emails in exercise 4.1 using less formal language.

A _____

_____

_____

_____

B _____

_____

_____

_____

7 Writing task

1 Work with a partner to arrange a meeting. Decide who is A and who is B, then complete the chart below. You can use true and / or imaginary information.

	Student A	Student B
name		
company		
you want to discuss		
level of formality	☐ formal ☐ informal	

2 Follow the flow chart and exchange emails with your partner.

1 Write an email to your partner.
 – suggest meeting
 – mention the topic you want to discuss
 – suggest a time and place to meet

2 Exchange emails.

3 Respond to your partner's email.
 – refuse politely
 – suggest another time / place

4 Exchange emails.

5 Respond. Agree with the new time / place.

6 Exchange emails.

7 Change the arrangements for the meeting.

8 Exchange emails.

9 Respond to the change in the arrangements.

10 Exchange emails.

3 Discussing travel plans

IN THIS UNIT, YOU WILL LEARN HOW TO ...

▶ write about travel plans

▶ make polite requests about travel plans

▶ promise to do something

▶ write an itinerary

1 A visit to Japan

1 Number the emails below 1–4 in the correct order.

A ☐

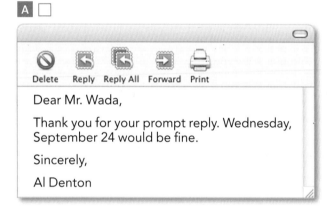

Dear Mr. Wada,

Thank you for your prompt reply. Wednesday, September 24 would be fine.

Sincerely,

Al Denton

B ☐

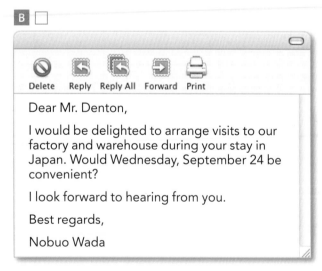

Dear Mr. Denton,

I would be delighted to arrange visits to our factory and warehouse during your stay in Japan. Would Wednesday, September 24 be convenient?

I look forward to hearing from you.

Best regards,

Nobuo Wada

C ☐

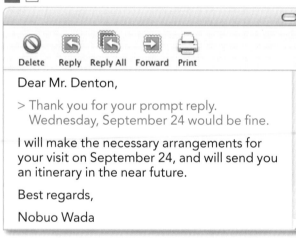

Dear Mr. Denton,

> Thank you for your prompt reply. Wednesday, September 24 would be fine.

I will make the necessary arrangements for your visit on September 24, and will send you an itinerary in the near future.

Best regards,

Nobuo Wada

D ☐

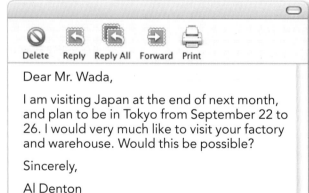

Dear Mr. Wada,

I am visiting Japan at the end of next month, and plan to be in Tokyo from September 22 to 26. I would very much like to visit your factory and warehouse. Would this be possible?

Sincerely,

Al Denton

2 Fill in the blanks using the information in the emails.

    a Mr. Denton is visiting Japan in _____ .

    b He plans to be in Tokyo for _____ days.

    c He wants to visit Mr. Wada's _____ .

    d Mr. Wada suggests September _____ .

    e Mr. Wada will send an _____ in the near future.

    f Mr. Wada uses the _____ function in his final email.

2 Writing about definite plans

1

To write about definite plans, you can use the present continuous tense:

I am visiting Japan next month.
We are touring the factory on Monday.

Note: do not use the present continuous tense with *be*:

~~I am being in Seoul next week.~~

You can also use *plan to (do)*:

Ms. Kim plans to visit Madrid in March.
I plan to be in Tokyo on Friday.

You can use a time phrase to write about definite plans:

next week / month   on Monday   in July   during my stay

Write sentences using the cues below.

a I / visit / Baltimore / in August

_____

b We / be / in Korea / for four days

_____

c They / inspect / the new plant / tomorrow

_____

d I / meet the R&D team / during my visit

_____

e Mr. Endo / be in Brazil / next week

_____

2 Write two sentences about your own definite plans.

_____

_____

_____

_____

_____

_____

_____

3 Making polite requests

LANGUAGE FOCUS

You can talk about your plans and make a polite request like this:

I am visiting Delhi next month. I would like to discuss the sales forecasts. Would this be possible?

You can combine the first and second sentences with _and_ like this:

I am visiting Delhi next month _and_ would like to discuss the sales forecasts. Would this be possible?

Write sentences with _and_, using the cues below.

a visit Hong Kong in May / discuss restructuring

b arrive at the office at around 10 a.m. / meet Ms. Chang

c bring / the plans of the new plant / discuss them with the architects

d be in Cairo next month / visit our suppliers

e meet the research team in May / give a presentation on future plans

4 Promising

LANGUAGE FOCUS

When you promise to do something, use:

I	will	send you	a proposed	immediately.
We		provide you with	itinerary	in the next few days.
				as soon as possible.
				before your departure.
				by April 23.
		let you know	a possible	
		inform you of	date	

Rewrite the words in the correct order. Pay attention to capital letters and punctuation.

a an itinerary of / I will / you / your visit / later today / email

b as soon as possible / let you know / we will / a possible date

c recommended hotels / send / in the next few days / a list of / I will / you

d provide / before / we will / you / a detailed itinerary / with / your departure

5 Writing task 1

TIP!

When you reply to an email, you can:

— open a new email message
— use the reply function, and include all of the other email
— use the reply function and include some of the other email

Look at page 112 for more information on using the reply function.

1 Work with a partner. You are going abroad in the near future. Write an email to a business acquaintance (your partner) about your plans and make a request. You can use Al Denton's first email in exercise 1 as a model. Use the ideas below or your own ideas.

Mexico / Mexico City / meet the sales staff

Australia / Melbourne / attend a training course

Finland / Helsinki / tour the new plant

2 Exchange emails with your partner. Write a response to your partner's email. You can use Mr. Wada's first email in exercise 1 as a model.

3 Exchange emails again with your partner and write a response.

4 Exchange emails once more. Write a final response.

6 An itinerary

1 Read the email and itinerary Nobuo Wada prepared for Al Denton.

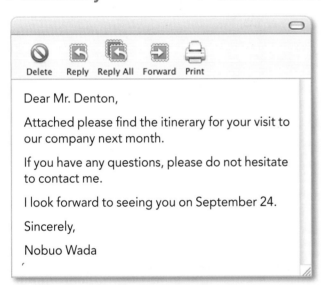

Delete   Reply   Reply All   Forward   Print

Dear Mr. Denton,

Attached please find the itinerary for your visit to our company next month.

If you have any questions, please do not hesitate to contact me.

I look forward to seeing you on September 24.

Sincerely,

Nobuo Wada

Al Denton: Itinerary, Tuesday, September 24

8:30 a.m.	Meet Etsuko Noda in Metropolitan Hotel lobby Taxi to Extec factory
9:30–11:30 a.m.	Factory tour
12:00–12.45 a.m.	Lunch in factory cafeteria with quality control supervisors
1:00–2:00 p.m.	Meeting with factory manager
2:00 p.m.	Car to warehouse
2:30–4:00 p.m.	Warehouse tour
4:00 p.m.	Refreshments
5:00 p.m.	Taxi to hotel (journey time approx. 45 minutes)
7:30 p.m.	Meet Nobuo Wada in lobby
8:00 p.m.	Dinner with senior managers

2 Are these statements about the itinerary true (T) or false (F)? Check (✓) the correct box.

	T	F
a The factory tour is in the afternoon.	☐	☐
b They are having lunch at the factory.	☐	☐
c There is a two-hour meeting in the afternoon.	☐	☐
d The warehouse tour takes 90 minutes.	☐	☐
e Mr. Denton has some free time before dinner.	☐	☐
f Ms. Noda is meeting Mr. Denton in the lobby at 7:30 p.m.	☐	☐

7 Writing an itinerary

LANGUAGE FOCUS

When you write an itinerary in simple note form, you only need to use important words. You can often omit:
— the subject *you*
— punctuation, e.g., periods
— articles (*a*, *an*, *the*) and some verbs:
  ~~have~~ lunch / dinner
  ~~give a~~ presentation / ~~take a~~ taxi / ~~make a~~ tour
  ~~go~~ to ~~the~~ convention center
  ~~attend a~~ concert / baseball game / exhibition / meeting

Write times on the left:
8:00 a.m., 10:30 a.m., 2:00 p.m., 4:30 p.m., 11:00 p.m.

To show a period of time, use a dash to connect two times:
10:00 a.m. – 11:00, 2:30 – 4:00 p.m. (approx.) *
*(approx. = approximately)

EXAMPLES   You are meeting Nobuo Wada in the Metropolitan Hotel lobby at 8:30.

8:30 a.m.   Meet Nobuo Wada in Metropolitan Hotel lobby

You are having refreshments in the company cafeteria at 4 p.m.

4:00 p.m.   Refreshments in company cafeteria

Wendy Koch is on a business trip to New York. Her clients have arranged to entertain her on Saturday. Rewrite the sentences below in itinerary style and complete the itinerary below.

a   You're meeting Nancy Monroe in the Sheraton Hotel lobby at 9:30 a.m.
b   You're going by taxi to the Museum of Modern Art at 9:45 a.m.
c   You're going to the Museum of Modern Art from 10 a.m. to 11:30 a.m.
d   You're having lunch with Nancy Monroe at 12:30 p.m. at La Toscana.
e   You're taking the ferry to the Statue of Liberty at 2:30 p.m.
f   You're meeting Fernando Lopez at Carnegie Hall at 7:30 p.m.
g   You're attending a jazz concert from 8 p.m. to 9:30 p.m. as the guest of Fisher Associates.
h   You're having a late dinner at the Blue Note at 10:30 p.m.

9:30 a.m. Meet Nancy Monroe in Sheraton Hotel lobby

_____

_____

_____

_____

_____

_____

_____

8 Writing task 2

Work with a partner. Write an itinerary for a two-day visit by a foreign guest to your company or school. Your itinerary should include one day of business-related activities and one day of sightseeing / entertainment. You can use the ideas below or your own ideas.

a   meet at ...

b   meet in ...

c   taxi to ...

d   train to ...

e   tour of ...

f   meeting with ...

g   lunch with ...

h   give a presentation

i   visit ...

j   make a speech

k   dinner with ...

l   free time

4 Recommending

▶ write about indefinite plans

▶ ask for recommendations

▶ make recommendations

1 An email to a business acquaintance

1 Read this email from a Japanese businessman to an American business acquaintance. Is the email formal or informal?

To: Frank Yarina <fyarina@insel.com>

Cc:

Subject: Possible trip to San Francisco

Dear Frank,

How are things with you?

It's not for sure yet, but I'm probably visiting San Francisco in July, and I hope we can meet to talk about the new project. I'll let you know as soon as I have some dates.

I'd like to stay at a reasonably-priced hotel. Do you have any recommendations? Also, do you have any suggestions for sightseeing?

Looking forward to hearing from you.

Best wishes,

Tetsuo

2 Complete the questions.

a _____ is Tetsuo writing to?
   He's writing to Frank.

b _____ is Tetsuo writing?
   To tell Frank about his plans.

c _____ is Tetsuo probably visiting the U.S.?
   In July.

d _____ does he ask Frank to recommend?
   Hotels and sightseeing.

2 Writing about indefinite plans

LANGUAGE FOCUS

In Unit 3, we used the present continuous tense to write about definite future arrangements:

I'm *visiting* the U.S. in July.

If you are less certain, you can add *probably*:

I'm *probably* visiting the U.S. in July.

If you are even less certain, you can use *might be* + *ing*:

I *might be visiting* the U.S. in July.

When you are uncertain about your future plans, you can also use these phrases:

	but		
It's not definite yet,	but	I'm probably visiting	the U.S. in July.
It's not decided yet,		I might be visiting	
It's not for sure yet,			

Rewrite these sentences using *probably* or *might*. Use the above phrases, too.

a   I'm meeting the designer next Friday.

_____

b   We're staying at the Sheraton.

_____

c   We're signing the contract Monday morning.

_____

d   They're arriving at 11 a.m.

_____

e   She's flying with American Airlines.

_____

2   Write two sentences about your own indefinite plans (business and / or social).

a   _____

_____

b   _____

_____

3 Asking for recommendations

You can ask for recommendations like this:

I would like to stay at a reasonably-priced hotel near the main offices.	Do you have any recommendations? What would you recommend? Do you have any suggestions?
Can you recommend Do you know	a reasonably-priced hotel near the station? a good place to buy a digital video camera?

You are visiting a foreign city on business in the near future. Ask a business acquaintance there to make a recommendation for each situation below. Use a different expression each time.

a (find) a good vegetarian restaurant

b (stay) at a quiet hotel near the city center

c (use) a reliable translation agency

d (buy) some souvenirs for my family

e your own idea

a _____

_____

b _____

_____

c _____

_____

d _____

_____

e _____

_____

4 Writing task 1

Frank Yarina is probably going to visit your city / town for the first time on business. He writes an email to a business acquaintance (think of a name) who knows the place well, asking for recommendations. Write the email. You can use Tetsuo's email in exercise 1 as a model.

5 A reply

1 Read Frank's reply to Tetsuo. Does Frank use the reply function?

To:	Tetsuo Tanaka
Cc:	
Subject:	RE: Possible trip to San Francisco

Dear Tetsuo,

> How are things with you?

Pretty good, thanks.

> It's not definite yet, but I'm probably visiting San Francisco in
> July, and I hope we can meet to talk about the new project. I'll
> let you know as soon as I have some dates.

Great. I hope you can make it.

> I would like to stay at a reasonably-priced hotel. Do you have
> any recommendations?

The Garden Hotel is very good, and it's a few minutes' walk from our office. The rates are very reasonable, too.

> Also, do you have any suggestions for sightseeing?

It depends on how much time you have. There are plenty of things to see in San Francisco, but if you have a couple of free days, you could make a trip to the Napa Valley; the vineyards are beautiful. If you have longer, then I recommend a drive to the Sierra Nevada mountains.

Let me know when you have some definite dates for your trip.

Best regards,

Frank

2 Write the words and phrases which mean the same or almost the same as the items below:

a you will be able to come _____
b near _____
c inexpensive _____
d a lot of _____
e have more time _____
f tell me _____

6 Recommending

You can recommend a company or service like this:

The Garden Hotel is	very good.
Brandt Associates are	excellent.

Dino's Restaurant has	a good reputation.
G.M.S. Electronics have	

I think the Park Avenue Hotel is very good.
I would recommend Dino's restaurant.

You can recommend a place like this:

Kyoto is		very interesting.
		definitely worth a visit.
You	should	visit Oxford, if you have time.
	could	
There are lots of		places to visit in Singapore.
		things to do in Boston.

Write recommendations for things that you know. Use a different expression each time.

a   a company

_____

b   a restaurant

_____

c   a sightseeing location

_____

d   a hotel

_____

7 Giving more information 1

When recommending something, you can add a reason, for example:

Sydney Harbor is definitely worth a visit; the Opera House is very impressive.

Le Chateau is good; they have an excellent wine list.

I would recommend Virgin Atlantic; the service is very good.

Match the company or service with the recommendation.

a	The City Art Gallery	1	They've worked on some great ad campaigns.
b	The Plaza Hotel	2	It has low rates and the latest models.
c	Orient Airways	3	They're very creative and their ideas are terrific.
d	The Web Design Company	4	It's one of the best places to stay in the city.
e	ACE Advertising	5	They have trained staff and all the latest exercise equipment.
f	Quantum Plastics	6	It's definitely worth a visit, it has some wonderful paintings.
g	Apex Car Rentals	7	The flights are nearly always on time.
h	Sweaters Sports Club	8	Their quality control team is excellent.

2 Choose three of the companies or services in 7.1 and write a sentence about each one similar to the sentences in the *Language focus* box.

_____

_____

_____

_____

_____

_____

8 Writing task 2

Work with a partner and exchange the emails you wrote in Writing task 1 (exercise 4). Write a reply and send it to your partner.

5 Inviting

IN THIS UNIT YOU WILL LEARN HOW TO ...

▸ write formal and informal invitations

▸ accept an invitation

▸ discuss likes and preferences

▸ refuse an invitation

1 Two invitations

1 Read the invitations. Which one is more formal? Why do you think so?

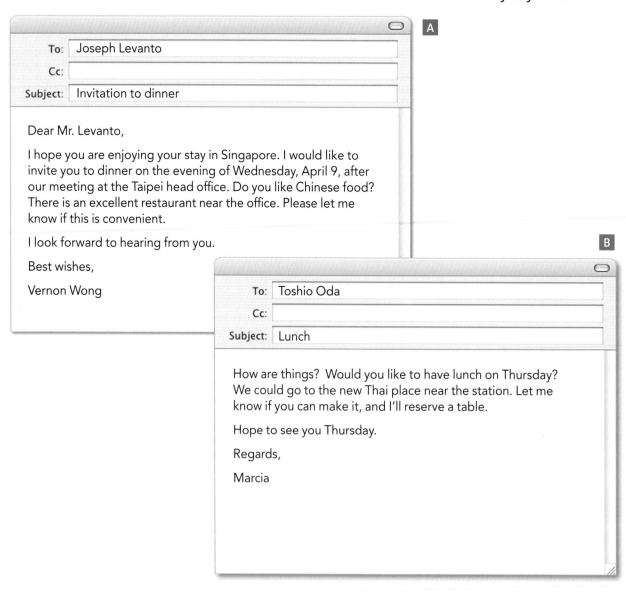

A

To: Joseph Levanto

Cc:

Subject: Invitation to dinner

Dear Mr. Levanto,

I hope you are enjoying your stay in Singapore. I would like to invite you to dinner on the evening of Wednesday, April 9, after our meeting at the Taipei head office. Do you like Chinese food? There is an excellent restaurant near the office. Please let me know if this is convenient.

I look forward to hearing from you.

Best wishes,

Vernon Wong

B

To: Toshio Oda

Cc:

Subject: Lunch

How are things? Would you like to have lunch on Thursday? We could go to the new Thai place near the station. Let me know if you can make it, and I'll reserve a table.

Hope to see you Thursday.

Regards,

Marcia

2 Are these statements about the invitations true (T) or false (F)?

		T	F
a	Mr. Levanto lives in Singapore.	☐	☐
b	Vernon Wong invites Mr. Levanto to dinner.	☐	☐
c	Mr. Levanto should contact Vernon Wong about the invitation.	☐	☐
d	Marcia invites Toshio to dinner on Friday.	☐	☐
e	Marcia suggests a Thai restaurant.	☐	☐
f	Toshio doesn't need to contact her about the invitation.	☐	☐

2 Inviting

You can write a polite invitation like this:

| Would you like to join | me | for lunch on Friday? |
| How about joining | us | |

| Would you like to | tour the factory after our meeting? |
| | do some sightseeing on the weekend? |

For a more formal invitation, write:

I		would like to	a party on Friday,
My wife and I		invite you to	June 10.
On behalf of	AK Computers, I the managing director,	we	the opening of our new branch on Wednesday, May 5.

Fill in the blanks to complete these invitations.

a   I would _____ to _____ you to lunch at the Imperial Hotel before you leave.

b   _____ you like _____ visit our R&D Department after your presentation?

c   How _____ _____ me for a round of golf on Saturday?

d   _____ _____ _____ the Accounting Department, I would like to invite you to an informal party on March 31 to mark your retirement.

3 Asking about likes and preferences

When you write an invitation, you may need to check a person's likes and preferences. Match the phrases on the left with the phrases on the right.

a	Do you like	1	any dietary restrictions.
b	Please let me know if you have	2	acceptable?
c	Do you have	3	you don't like?
d	Is there any kind of food	4	sukiyaki?
e	Is traditional Japanese seating	5	any preferences?

4 Opening and concluding an invitation

1 You can use sentences like the ones below to open and conclude an invitation. Which sentences are opening sentences (O)? Which are concluding sentences (C)? Which can be both? Check (✓) the correct box(es).

		O	C
a	Please let me know if you can attend.	☐	☐
b	I hope you are enjoying your stay in Korea.	☐	☐
c	I look forward to hearing from you.	☐	☐
d	Thank you for your email.	☐	☐
e	I hope to see you soon.	☐	☐
f	I hope you are well.	☐	☐

2 The sentences below are less formal. Match them with the sentences in exercise 1, writing the correct letter (a, b, etc.) in the box. What makes them less formal? Look at the *Language focus* box on page 14 if you need help.

1 See you soon! ☐
2 Thanks for your email. ☐
3 Look forward to hearing from you. ☐
4 Let me know if you can make it. ☐
5 Hope you're enjoying your stay. ☐
6 How are you? ☐

5 Writing task 1

Work with a partner. You should each choose a different situation, A or B. Write an invitation for your situation. Use the emails in exercise 1.1 as models.

SITUATION A
Yvonne Artaud, a French businesswoman, is visiting your country to do business with your company. You have met only once before, in France last year. She took you to an excellent restaurant in Paris. You invite her to dinner at a restaurant in your town / city. Think of a restaurant you know or use the ideas below. Choose a day and date.

Indian

Italian

Japanese

your idea

SITUATION B
Luigi Ponti, an Italian businessman, is visiting your country to do business with your company. You have met many times before and often communicate by email. He has visited your country a number of times, and has seen the major sightseeing spots. Invite him to do something this Saturday. Think of your own idea or use the ideas below.

golf

art gallery

shopping

your idea

6 Accepting an invitation

LANGUAGE FOCUS

To accept a formal invitation, you can say:

Thank you very much for your kind invitation.	I would be delighted to	join you for dinner. attend the party.

If the invitation is informal, respond like this:

Thanks for the invitation.	Dinner on Friday would be great. I'd love to have dinner.

Rewrite the words in the correct order. There are two sentences in each example. Pay attention to capital letters and punctuation.

a   April 6 / your kind invitation / on / would be delighted / thank you very much / to come to / Saturday / for / I / your party

_____

_____

b   a round of golf / thanks / for / to join you / for / on the weekend / I'd love / the invitation

_____

_____

7 Responding about likes and preferences

1

LANGUAGE FOCUS

To describe likes and preferences, you can use:

I love sukiyaki.	I'm afraid I don't care for sukiyaki, but I do like tempura.
I like Italian food very much. Any kind of food will be fine. Traditional Japanese seating would be fine.	I'm allergic to (fish). I'm a vegetarian. I'd prefer to sit at a table, if possible.

Match the questions you wrote in exercise 3 with one or two of the answers above.

2   Answer the questions you wrote in exercise 3 using information about you.

a   _____

_____

b   _____

_____

c   _____

_____

d   _____

_____

e   _____

_____

LANGUAGE FOCUS

To refuse a formal invitation, you can write:

Thank you very much for your kind invitation.	I'm afraid Unfortunately,	I have an appointment on that day. I have already made arrangements for that date. I am unable to attend.

You can add:

Please accept my apologies.
I hope you have a wonderful evening.

You can refuse an informal invitation like this:

Thanks for the invitation.	I'm sorry, but	I can't make it I'm busy	Thursday evening.
		I'll be out of town on Thursday. I have to work late on Friday.	

You can add:

Maybe some other time?
Have a great time!

Rewrite the sentences in the correct order. There are three sentences in each example. Pay attention to capital letters and punctuation.

a   I have / my apologies / your kind invitation / please accept / already made / arrangements / thank you very much for / I'm afraid / for April 6

_____

_____

_____

_____

_____

b   the invitation / out of town / but I'll be / I'm sorry / some other time / on the weekend / maybe / thanks for

_____

_____

_____

_____

_____

2 Write the sentences below in the correct order to make two different responses to the emails in exercise 1.1. One email accepts the invitation and the other refuses. Write the emails below.

a   I love Chinese food – in fact, it's my favorite.
b   Maybe some other time?
c   I look forward to meeting you in Taiwan.
d   I would be delighted to have dinner on Wednesday evening after the meeting.
e   I'm having lunch with a client that day.
f   Thank you very much for your kind invitation.
g   Thanks for the invitation.
h   I'm sorry, but I can't make it on Thursday.

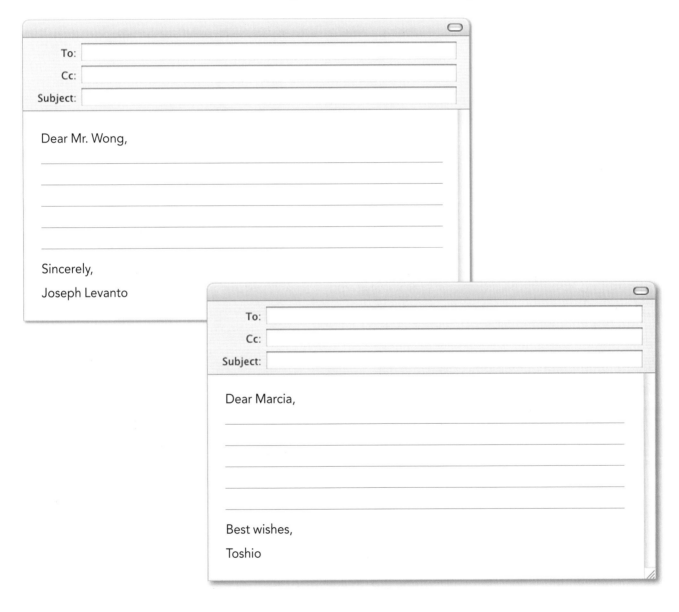

To:

Cc:

Subject:

Dear Mr. Wong,

Sincerely,

Joseph Levanto

To:

Cc:

Subject:

Dear Marcia,

Best wishes,

Toshio

9 Writing task 2 Exchange the invitations you and your partner wrote in Writing task 1 (exercise 5) and respond by email. One of you should accept the invitation and the other should refuse. Toss a coin to decide.

Review 1

1 An email to a business acquaintance

1 Read the email quickly. Petra Lundhof has two main reasons for writing to Mr. Chen. What are they?

Delete Reply Reply All Forward Print

Dear Mr. Chen,

This is a brief email to introduce myself. I am the new operations manager at Storage Solutions. Previously I was assistant operations manager in the Chicago office but moved to corporate headquarters last month. I am replacing John Wicks, who is now operations director.

Let me tell you a little about myself. I joined Storage Solutions ten years ago. Before that I worked for a software company. My background is in software development and project management.

I am now responsible for John's projects. I wonder if we could arrange a teleconference sometime soon to discuss these projects? I'm available any time next week.

I hope to hear from you soon and look forward to working with you.

Sincerely,

Petra Lundhof

2 Complete the questions.

a Who is _____?
  She's the new operations manager.

b When did she _____?
  Last month.

c When did she _____?
  Ten years ago.

d Where did she _____?
  At a software company.

e Why does she _____?
  She wants to discuss the projects.

f When is she _____?
  Any time next week.

3 Now write Mr. Chen's reply to Petra Lundhof. Use the notes below to help you or use your own ideas.

> thank Ms. Lundhof for her email – happy to discuss the projects with her – suggest a day and time next week

2 Word puzzle

Write the answers to the clues below in the puzzle. When you have finished, read down to find the missing word in this sentence:

Can you _____ a good hotel in New York?

a When you're in Amsterdam, go to the Van Gogh Museum. It's definitely w _____ a visit.

b I don't eat meat. I'm a v _____ .

c If you have any questions, please get in t _____ with me.

d If you want to change the arrangements for a meeting, you should a _____ and suggest another time and place.

e *Punctual* means "on t _____ ".

f Tea, coffee, and snacks are examples of r _____ .

g I can't eat seafood – it makes me sick. I'm a _____ to it.

h If you refuse an invitation you usually give a r _____ .

i Another word for *now* is "i _____ ".

3 Formal and informal

Rewrite these sentences in a more polite, more formal way.

a I want to have a meeting with you sometime next week.

_____

b How about dinner on Friday?

_____

c See you at the trade fair on Monday.

_____

d You can call me any time.

_____

e I can't come to the sales conference next month. I'm busy.

_____

f I want to visit your new factory. Is this O.K.?

_____

Rewrite these sentences in a polite but less formal way.

g Thank you for your kind invitation.

_____

h I would be delighted to attend the party.

_____

i Please accept my sincere apologies.

_____

j Unfortunately, a meeting on January 2 would be inconvenient for me.

_____

4 Pairwork dictation

1 Work with a partner. Take turns reading sentences to your partner, who will write them down.
Student A: Use the sentences on page 109.
Student B: Use the sentences on page 110.

> **LANGUAGE FOCUS**
>
> Could you say that again?
> Could you speak more slowly?
> How do you spell "…"?
> What's the (fourth) word?

Now write the sentences that your partner reads out to you.

a _____

b _____

c _____

d _____

e _____

f _____

2 When you have finished, compare your sentences with your partner's page. Did you spell everything correctly?

5 Correct the mistakes

REMEMBER!

Before you send an email or letter, always check for mistakes in:
— capitalization
— spelling
— punctuation
— grammar
— vocabulary
(Look at pages 124–128 for more information.)

Below is the first draft of an email message about a business trip to the U.S. There are two mistakes in each of the following:
— spelling
— punctuation
— capitalization
— verb tenses
— prepositions

Find the 10 mistakes and correct them.

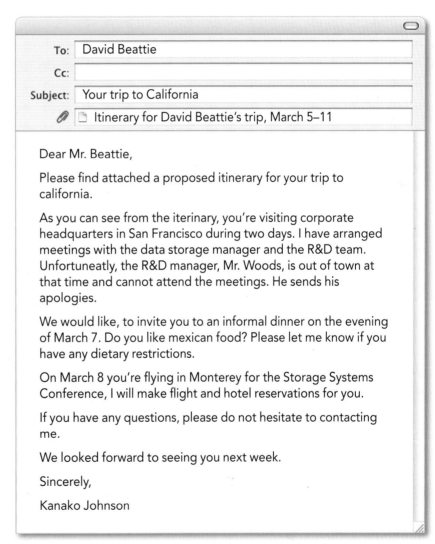

To: David Beattie

Cc:

Subject: Your trip to California

📎 🗎 Itinerary for David Beattie's trip, March 5–11

Dear Mr. Beattie,

Please find attached a proposed itinerary for your trip to california.

As you can see from the iterinary, you're visiting corporate headquarters in San Francisco during two days. I have arranged meetings with the data storage manager and the R&D team. Unfortuneatly, the R&D manager, Mr. Woods, is out of town at that time and cannot attend the meetings. He sends his apologies.

We would like, to invite you to an informal dinner on the evening of March 7. Do you like mexican food? Please let me know if you have any dietary restrictions.

On March 8 you're flying in Monterey for the Storage Systems Conference, I will make flight and hotel reservations for you.

If you have any questions, please do not hesitate to contacting me.

We looked forward to seeing you next week.

Sincerely,

Kanako Johnson

6 Making inquiries

> **IN THIS UNIT YOU WILL LEARN HOW TO ...**
>
> ▶ write an email inquiring about products or services
>
> ▶ give a reason for writing
>
> ▶ write a short description of your company
>
> ▶ describe your interest in a product or service
>
> ▶ request a catalog, price list, sample, etc.

1 An inquiry

1 Read the email to a machine manufacturer quickly. What does Etsuko want the company to send? Check (✓) the correct box.

a machinery ☐
b information ☐
c plastic household goods ☐

To: www.marketing@wesplas.com
Cc:
Subject: Catalog request

Dear Wesplas:

We saw your advertisement in Plastics Monthly and would like to know more about your molding machines.

As you may know, Plascom is a successful manufacturer of high quality plastic household goods with an extensive sales network throughout East and South East Asia. We are planning to replace our molding machines in the near future.

Would you please send us your latest catalog, including a full price list and details of discounts. Please send them to the address below.

I look forward to hearing from you.

Sincerely,

Etsuko Goto
Assistant Production Controller
Plascom
1–30–6 Nishi Gotanda
Shinagawa-ku
Tokyo 142–8436
Japan

2 Answer the questions.

a Why doesn't Etsuko write a person's name in the salutation?

b In which magazine did she see the advertisement?

c What does her company make?

d What exactly does she ask the company to send?

2 Organizing your ideas

1 Fill in the blanks in the email. Use the words below.

interested   know   hope   send   supplier   details

To: info@ezklene.com

Cc:

Subject: Catalog and price list

Dear EZKlene,

I visited your stand at the Frankfurt Office Automation Show last week and would like to ¹ _____ more about your latest detergent products.

Our company is a fast-growing ² _____ of office-cleaning services with branches all over Germany. We are very ³ _____ in importing your products into this country.

Would you please ⁴ _____ us your latest catalog, including a full price list and ⁵ _____ of wholesale discounts. Please send them to the address below.

I ⁶ _____ to hear from you soon.

Sincerely,

Kurt Bleiberg
Manager
Import Department
R.G. Ibbeken AG
Klosterstr. 85
40231 Düsseldorf
Germany

---

2 When you write an email or letter, always organize your ideas carefully in paragraphs. Number these items 1–4 to match the order of the paragraphs in Kurt Bleiburg's email above.

Kurt …

☐ gives a brief description of his company and explains his interest in EZKlene's products

☐ writes a polite ending

☐ says why he is writing

☐ asks EZKlene to send some information

3 Giving a reason for writing

1

You can give a reason for writing like this:

| We saw | your company's stand at the Furniture Fair in Stockholm last week. |
| | your advertisement in the October issue of *Furniture Monthly*. |

I recently saw your company's website on the Internet.
We were given your name by Hendrik Larssen of IKEA.

We are very interested in	your	products.
I would like to know more about	your company's	services.
		new lines.
We would like to receive some information about		

You can combine the sentences with *and*:

We saw your company's stand at the Furniture Fair in Stockholm last week.
+ *and* +
We are very interested in your products.

If both parts have the same subject (e.g. *we*), you can omit the subject the second time:

We saw your company's stand at the Furniture Fair in Stockholm last week *and* (we) are very interested in your products.

Combine two pairs of other sentences in the table in the same way.

a _____

_____

b _____

_____

2 Work with a partner. Write a similar sentence giving a reason for writing to a company of your choice.

_____

_____

LANGUAGE FOCUS

1 To describe your company you can use:

Our company Kite	is a	small medium -sized large fast -growing major	manufacturer importer distributor supplier retailer	of	ball-bearings. sportswear.
			budget hotel chain.		
		well-known successful	supplier provider	of	office -cleaning accounting services.

We have	an excellent reputation all over East Asia.
	branches throughout the Tokyo area.
	factories in Beijing and Manila.
	offices in Japan, the United States, and Canada.
	an extensive sales network throughout the U.K.

You can combine the sentences above, using *with*, like this:

Our company is a large manufacturer of ball-bearings.
+ *with* +
We have factories in Beijing and Manila.

Our company is a large manufacturer of ball-bearings with factories in Beijing and Manila.

TIP!
If you think the reader may know your company, you can begin with one of these phrases:
As you may know, . . .
You may know that . . .
You may be aware that . . .

Write similar sentences about your own company and / or a company you know.

a _____

_____

b _____

_____

2 Work with a partner. Write a sentence about an imaginary company and present your information to the class.

_____

_____

5 Describing your interest in a product or service

1

You can say why you are interested in a company's products or services like this:

We are looking for a new supplier of office equipment.

We are interested in We are considering	retailing your products in Canada. changing our catering service.

We are planning to extend our factory space in the near future.

Write similar sentences using these ideas. Add words and change the verb form where necessary. Pay attention to capitalization and punctuation.

a we / interested / import / your products / to Korea

b we / plan / replace / I.T. system / next year

c we / look for / distributor for our products / U.S.

d we / consider / expand / product line

2 Work with a partner. Write two sentences using your own ideas about your own and / or an imaginary company.

a

b

6 Requests

1

You can make requests using these phrases:

Please Would you please We would appreciate it if you would	send us let us have provide us with	your current catalog. your latest price list. details of your services. information on your new products.

Rewrite these requests in the correct order. Pay attention to punctuation and capitalization.

a catalog / please / next / us / for / your / year / send

b discounts / you / wholesale / us / would / let / of / have / please / details

_____

_____

c appreciate / we / samples / provide / it / if / would / would / us / you some / with

_____

_____

2 Work with a partner. Write a request using your own ideas.

_____

_____

7 Writing task

1 Work with a partner. Complete the notes below about a real or imaginary company.

Name:

Location – Country:
             City:

Products / Services:

Reason for writing:

Please send:

2 Exchange notes with another pair of students. Write an inquiry email to the company they wrote about. You can write as an employee of your own company or an imaginary company.

EPSON
Organic Light Emitting Display

7 Placing orders

1 Two orders

1 Read the two emails quickly. What products are they ordering?

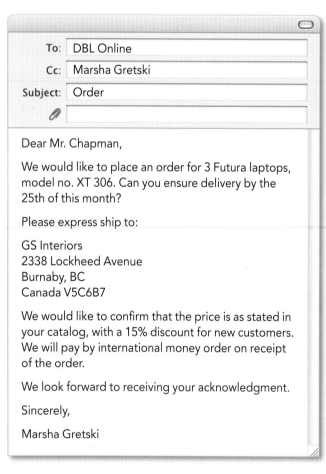

To:	DBL Online
Cc:	Marsha Gretski
Subject:	Order
📎	

Dear Mr. Chapman,

We would like to place an order for 3 Futura laptops, model no. XT 306. Can you ensure delivery by the 25th of this month?

Please express ship to:

GS Interiors
2338 Lockheed Avenue
Burnaby, BC
Canada V5C6B7

We would like to confirm that the price is as stated in your catalog, with a 15% discount for new customers. We will pay by international money order on receipt of the order.

We look forward to receiving your acknowledgment.

Sincerely,

Marsha Gretski

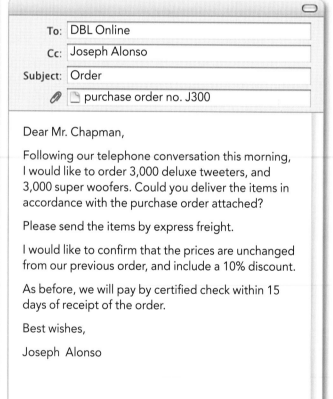

To:	DBL Online
Cc:	Joseph Alonso
Subject:	Order
📎	📄 purchase order no. J300

Dear Mr. Chapman,

Following our telephone conversation this morning, I would like to order 3,000 deluxe tweeters, and 3,000 super woofers. Could you deliver the items in accordance with the purchase order attached?

Please send the items by express freight.

I would like to confirm that the prices are unchanged from our previous order, and include a 10% discount.

As before, we will pay by certified check within 15 days of receipt of the order.

Best wishes,

Joseph Alonso

2 Check (✓) the correct column to answer the questions.

Who . . .	Ms. Gretski	Mr. Alonso
a gives a delivery date?	☐	☐
b is a new customer?	☐	☐
c discussed the order on the phone?	☐	☐
d asks for the goods to be express shipped?	☐	☐
e will pay by certified check?	☐	☐
f will pay by international money order?	☐	☐
g attaches a purchase order?	☐	☐

2 Ordering and delivery

1

When placing an order the following are useful:

I We	would like to	place an order for order	six office chairs, 500 deluxe tweeters,	model part item	no. T50.	
Can Could	you	deliver the	items goods order	by before	March 14	?
					the 25th of this week the end of this month	
Please		ensure delivery			next month	.

Write two sentences for each order below. Use different expressions each time.

a

> 200 pairs of Fasta jogging
> shoes / model no. F342 /
> (delivery – by June 10)

_____

_____

_____

b

> ten dining table sets /
> model no. JS700-2 /
> (delivery – before the end
> of February)

_____

_____

_____

2 Write a similar order using your own ideas or the ideas below.

_____

_____

_____

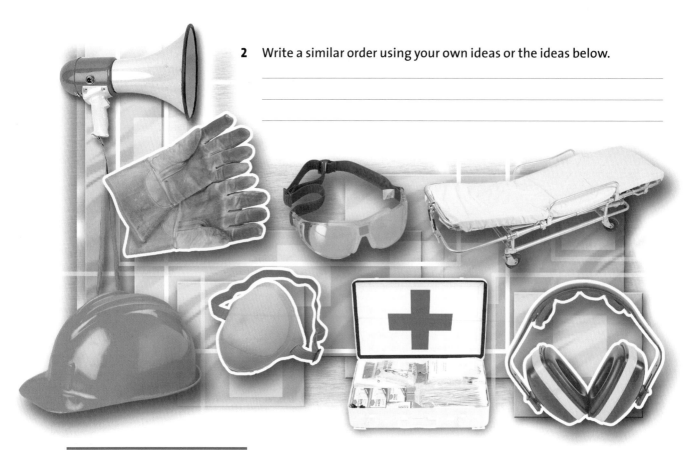

3 Methods of delivery

1 Match each phrase with the correct picture.

rail   sea   air   ground   express delivery

2 Complete the sentences with an appropriate method of delivery. There may be more than one correct answer for each sentence.

a   30 tons of cement
Please send the shipment by _____ .

b   6 valuable original paintings for the head office
Please send the items via* _____ .

*_via_ means the same as "by".

c   20 cases of caviar from overseas – urgent
Please send the shipment by _____ .

d   20 secondhand cars from a foreign country.
Please send the shipment via _____ .

1

To discuss price and payment, you can use:

We would like to confirm that	the price is $10 per item.
	we will receive a 10% discount.
	the prices are unchanged from our previous order.

We will	pay	by	certified check.
As agreed, we will	make payment		international money order.
		in advance.	
		on	receipt of the goods.
		within 30 days of	order. invoice.

Fill in the blanks in the text below using the words in the *Language focus* box above.

We would like to ¹ _____ that the price is $250
² _____ item, and that we will ³ _____
a 15% discount. We will make ⁴ _____ by
international money ⁵ _____ , and as
⁶ _____ , will pay on ⁷ _____ of the
goods.

2   Write similar sentences using this information.

confirm price / $39.49 per item / 10% discount / pay by certified check / pay on receipt of invoice

_____

_____

_____

_____

5 Placing a large order

When you place an order by email, letter, or fax, include all the important information, e.g.,
— a list of the items your are ordering (quantity, description, unit price)
— when you want to receive the order
— the shipping address (the address the goods should be shipped to)
— how you want the order shipped (air, sea, express mail, etc.)
— total amount due
— payment method (certified check, international money order)

1   You can write an email, letter, or fax to place a simple order, as in the emails in exercise 1. But if you are ordering a number of different items, make a list. Read the order below and answer the questions.

a   Who is placing the order?
b   What kind of item is she ordering?
c   How many does she order?
d   When does she want the item shipped?

Odd Moments

250 156th St.   Flushing, NY 11356
Phone: 718-357-7251   Fax: 718-357-7282
Email: oddmoments@aol.com

Dear Mr. Mankell,

Please accept this order for immediate shipment to the above address and charge it to our account # 4462.

Quantity	Model no.	Description	Unit Price	Total
100	TS530	Penguin Lamps	$5.25	$525.00
50	TS221	Hamster Lamps	$4.75	$237.50

We look forward to receiving your acknowledgement.

Sincerely,

Monica Hagen

Monica Hagen

2   Write a similar order using this information and your own company / school address.

to Ms. Delaney / immediate shipment / our account no. 2136 / 25 computer monitors (model no. ZX256) unit price $850.00 / 10 laser printers (model no. RP721-06) unit price $350.00 / 6 scanners (model no. J430) unit price $250.00

6 A purchase order

1 Most companies use their own purchase order form like the one below.

◻ Braddock Construction
386 Western Circle   Chicago, IL 60601

Purchase order

| 04-7100-3 |

Date: November 3, 2005

Requisitioned by: Nick Weng

Issued to:	**Ship via:** ground
Donovan Construction Supplies Inc. 153 S Main St Collierville, TN 38017 Telephone: 901-851-9453 Fax: 901-851-9454 Email: orders@donovansupplies.com	**Ship to:** Braddock factory, Western Circle Chicago IL 60601 **Ship by (date):** November 10, 2005

QUANTITY	DESCRIPTION	UNIT PRICE	TOTAL
36 tubes	Kwikstik Polyurethane Glue (Item # KS276)	$6.95	$250.20
48 bottles	Kwikstick Wood Glue (Item # KS214)	$9.99	$479.52
48 cartridges	Kwikstik Heavy Duty Adhesive (Item # KS316)	$4.99	$239.52
		SUBTOTAL:	$969.24
		SALES TAX (8.75%):	$84.81
		SHIPPING & HANDLING:	$227.00
		TOTAL:	$1,281.05

Authorized by: Lois Van Dyke   **Date:** November 4, 2005

Are these statements about the purchase order true (T) or false (F)? Check the correct box.

		T	F
a	Braddock Construction is ordering the goods.	☐	☐
b	Nick Weng placed the order.	☐	☐
c	Lois Van Dyke approved the order.	☐	☐
d	The shipment will be sent by air.	☐	☐
e	The order is for four items.	☐	☐
f	The total amount is $1,350.	☐	☐

2 Your teacher will give you a blank order form. Complete it using this information, your own name, and the current date.

> You work for Braddock Construction. You want to order the following items from Donovan Construction Supplies: 10 model #400 windows (unit price $200), 4 model #250 windows (unit price $250), and 8 model #672 doors (unit price $225). Jay Obara will authorize the order. Sales tax is 8.75% of the subtotal.
>
> Shipping and handling will be $960.

7 A cover letter

Usually, you should mail a cover letter with a purchase order. Complete the cover letter using the words below.

receive   contact   process   confirm   find

VISTA LANDSCAPING

603 Fender Avenue
Trumbull, CT 06622
Tel: (203) 261-9946
Fax: (203) 261-8237
vistalandscape@aol.com

Dear Ms. Zabriskie,

Please ¹ _____ enclosed our purchase order no. #04-7100-5.

Please ² _____ that you can ³ _____ the order immediately.

We would like to ⁴ _____ the shipment by May 14.

If there are any problems, please feel free to ⁵ _____ me.

Sincerely yours,

Norman Judd

Norman Judd

8 Writing Task 1

Write a similar cover letter for the purchase order in exercise 6.1. Address it to Ms. Kruyt.

Write an email to ValuMart Office Supplies. Order one or more of the items below, or use your own ideas. Use your own name.

BERGSEN office chair

model no. N562

$800

FINMARK shredder

model no. J211

$375

KARIMA Coffee Maker

model no. K119

$150

WINDSOR NOTEBOOK CASE

model no. 4352

$34

8 Responding to orders

1 Two emails

1 Read the two emails quickly. Which order is a problem for Imrat Singh?

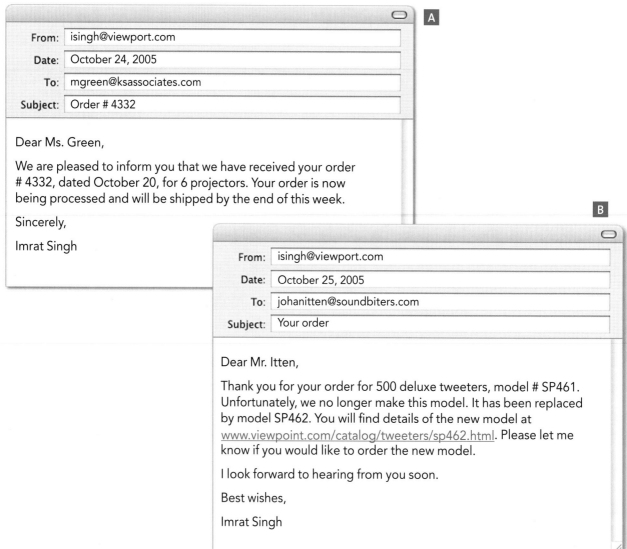

A

From:	isingh@viewport.com
Date:	October 24, 2005
To:	mgreen@ksassociates.com
Subject:	Order # 4332

Dear Ms. Green,

We are pleased to inform you that we have received your order # 4332, dated October 20, for 6 projectors. Your order is now being processed and will be shipped by the end of this week.

Sincerely,

Imrat Singh

B

From:	isingh@viewport.com
Date:	October 25, 2005
To:	johanitten@soundbiters.com
Subject:	Your order

Dear Mr. Itten,

Thank you for your order for 500 deluxe tweeters, model # SP461. Unfortunately, we no longer make this model. It has been replaced by model SP462. You will find details of the new model at www.viewpoint.com/catalog/tweeters/sp462.html. Please let me know if you would like to order the new model.

I look forward to hearing from you soon.

Best wishes,

Imrat Singh

2 Are these statements true (T) or false (F)? Check (✓) the boxes.

		T	F
a	Ms. Green's order is for 6 projectors.	☐	☐
b	There is a problem with Ms. Green's order.	☐	☐
c	Imrat wants Ms. Green to write to him.	☐	☐
d	Imrat is going to send Mr. Itten's shipment immediately.	☐	☐
e	Imrat's company no longer makes model no. SP461.	☐	☐
f	Imrat wants Mr. Itten to contact him.	☐	☐

2 Acknowledging an order

TIP!

You can use *the above order* if you have mentioned the order number in the subject line of your email or letter.

LANGUAGE FOCUS

When you acknowledge an order, these phrases are useful:

Thank you for		your order	no. 1230	of dated	June 10.
We are pleased to inform you that	we have received				for 3,000 tweeters.
We are pleased to confirm that This is to inform you that		the above order.			

Write a sentence to acknowledge each order below. Use a different expression each time.

a order no. B6299 / August 20

_____

_____

b order no. 2196 / 2,000 Star Ranger alarm clocks

_____

_____

c order no. X882 / 30 garden furniture sets
(You have mentioned the order number in the subject line of your email.)

_____

_____

3 Active vs. passive

LANGUAGE FOCUS

In business correspondence, the reader is often more interested in the action (what happens) than the agent (who does it). In this case, you can use the passive.

ACTIVE	PASSIVE
We are now processing your order.	Your order *is* now *being processed*.
We will pack the items in individual boxes.	The items *will be packed* in individual boxes.

Rewrite these sentences in the passive:

a   We are now putting together your order.

_____

b   We will ship your order immediately.

_____

c   We have discontinued this line.

_____

d   We have replaced this line with a new model.

_____

2   Look at email A in exercise 1.1. Write the sentence that combines these two shorter sentences:

Your order is now being processed.

Your order will be shipped by the end of this week.

_____

_____

3   Combine the sentences you wrote in exercise 3.1 in the same way.

sentences a and b

a   _____

_____

sentences c and d

b   _____

_____

4   Look again at email A in exercise 1.1 and write a similar message using the information below. Include a salutation and a complimentary closing, and use your own name.

To: Mr. Garcia / order no. 23886 / August 23 / gas ranges / model no. J6-304 / ship immediately

_____

_____

_____

4 Dealing with problems

LANGUAGE FOCUS

If there is a problem with shipping an order, you should write to the customer and:

— describe the problem
— if necessary, give a reason for the problem.

Unfortunately, We regret that We are sorry to inform you that	model no. X2334 the model you requested	has been discontinued. is out of stock at present.
	we no longer supply this model.	

		due to	
	your order will be delayed your order cannot be processed at present	due to	a fire at our factory. a mail strike. a computer network problem.

Write complete sentences using the ideas below and the above language. Use a different expression each time.

a problem at our new dispatch center

_____

_____

_____

b flood damage at our factory

_____

_____

_____

c model no. FF256 – discontinued

_____

_____

_____

5 Suggesting a solution

1 If necessary, you should also suggest a solution to the problem and write a polite ending to your message. Fill in the blanks in the sentences using the words below.

find   send   apologize   start   purchase   contact

1 We suggest that you _____ the new model. You will _____ details on page 49 of our catalog.

2 We will _____ you when the problem is resolved, and would like to _____ for any inconvenience.

3 We will _____ production again next week and will _____ your shipment as soon as possible.

2 Work with a partner. Match the 3 sentences above with the situations in exercise 4.

3 The underlined parts of the email below are not appropriate in polite business correspondence. Work with a partner and decide how to change them. Write the new sentences on the lines below. You can look at email B in exercise 1.1 to help you.

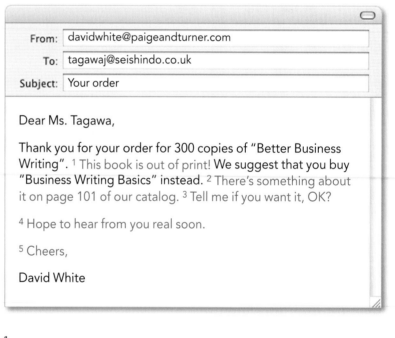

From: davidwhite@paigeandturner.com

To: tagawaj@seishindo.co.uk

Subject: Your order

Dear Ms. Tagawa,

Thank you for your order for 300 copies of "Better Business Writing". 1 This book is out of print! We suggest that you buy "Business Writing Basics" instead. 2 There's something about it on page 101 of our catalog. 3 Tell me if you want it, OK?

4 Hope to hear from you real soon.

5 Cheers,

David White

1 _____

2 _____

3 _____

4 _____

5 _____

6 Writing task **1** Write notes for an order on a piece of paper, as in this example:

Date:	November 11, 2005
Item:	Yazawa X-303 Electronic Drum Set Model # YH 2669
Quantity:	20
Signed:	*Gene Davis*

2 Exchange notes with a partner. Respond to your partner's order by email. Think of a reason why you cannot process the order immediately.

9 Making payment

IN THIS UNIT YOU WILL LEARN HOW TO ...

▶ inform someone about payment

▶ acknowledge payment

▶ remind someone about late payment

▶ use the first conditional in reminders

1 A letter to a supplier

1 Read the letter. Why is Mark Butler writing?

Thornton Engineering

www.thorntoneng.com

Re: Order # 32278

Dear Ms. Valdez:

Thank you for shipping the above order of machine parts, which arrived yesterday.

We would like to inform you that we have instructed our bank to transfer $2,479.00 to your account in payment of your invoice dated September 14. Could you please confirm that payment has been received?

I look forward to hearing from you.

Sincerely,

Mark Butler

Mark Butler

1694 Sherman Boulvard Suite 60 Denver, CO 80214
PHONE: (303) 825-4211   FAX: (303) 825-0726

2 Are these statements true (T) or false (F)?

		T	F
a	Mark Butler's company has bought something from Ms. Valdez's company.	☐	☐
b	Mark Butler's company has told its bank to pay some money into the account of Ms. Valdez's company.	☐	☐
c	The amount is more than $3,000.	☐	☐
d	The date on the invoice is September 4.	☐	☐
e	Mr. Butler wants Ms. Valdez to tell him when the money arrives.	☐	☐

3 Match the words and phrases on the left with the ones on the right that are the same or similar in meaning.

a	would like to inform you that	1	credit
b	we have instructed	2	has been completed
c	transfer	3	in settlement of
d	in payment of	4	notify us when
e	confirm that	5	we have authorized
f	has been made	6	are pleased to let you know that

4 Rewrite the main paragraph of the letter using the words and phrases on the right in exercise 3.

_____

_____

_____

_____

2 Acknowledging payment

1 Ms. Valdez wrote the letter below to Mr. Butler to say that her company had received payment. Complete the letter using the words below.

account   bank   business   certified check   payment
invoice   working

Dear Mr. Butler:

Our [1] _____ informed us yesterday that your
[2] _____ for $2,479.00 was credited to our
[3] _____ in [4] _____ of our
[5] _____ dated September 14.

Thank you for your [6] _____, and we look forward
to [7] _____ with you again.

Sincerely yours,

Anita Valdez

Anita Valdez

2 Write a similar letter to Heidi Frentzen using the information below. Use your own name.

bank informed us today – 5,000 euros transferred to our account – invoice dated March 2 – thank you

Dear ————————————————— ,

Our bank ———————————————————————

——————————————————————————

——————————————————————————

——————————————————————————

——————————————————————————

——————————————————————

———————————————

———————————

3 Writing task 1 **1** Work by yourself. Look at the letter in exercise 1.1. On a separate piece of paper write a similar letter to a supplier. Use the information below or your own ideas.

– write to Mr. Obata re. order
  no. 41160 (plastic sheeting)
– arrived this morning
– have instructed bank to transfer
  $1,435.50 to account
– invoice July 2
– confirm?

2 Exchange the letter you wrote in exercise 3.1 above with a partner. Write a reply to your partner's letter. You can use the letter in exercise 2.1 as a model.

4 A first reminder

1 **Read the letter from Ms. Valdez to another customer.**

a Why is she writing?

b Is the letter polite? How can you tell?

Dear Mr. Piaget:

This is a reminder that payment of invoice #3204 for our website design services is now one month overdue. We have attached a copy of the invoice for your reference.

We look forward to receiving payment in the near future.

Sincerely yours,

Anita Valdez

Anita Valdez

2 **Write the words or phrases in the letter which mean the same as ...**

a something that helps you to remember something _____

b late _____

c sent with the letter _____

d for you to look at _____

e very soon _____

3 **Write a similar letter to Ms. Wang, using the information below. Use your own name.**

to: Ms. Wang

re: invoice #44432

for: the shipment of 150 microscopes

overdue: ten days

_____

_____

_____

_____

_____

_____

_____

_____

_____

_____

5 A second reminder

1 Read Ms. Valdez's second reminder to Mr. Piaget. It was prepared by her new assistant. Is it polite?

> Louis,
>
> It's me again about the money for invoice #3204. Did you get my last letter (October 7)? You still owe us $204,321.59.
>
> I would love to get the money within five days (business days!) or sooner!
>
> Your friend,

2 Rearrange the items below to rewrite the letter above in an appropriate formal style. Pay attention to punctuation and capitalization.

The sum of $204,321.59 is still / Would you please / Sincerely yours, / In reference to / Anita Valdez / within five business days. / my letter of October 7, / outstanding. / about invoice #3204. / Dear Mr. Piaget, / reply or send us / a certified check in payment / I am writing again

_____

_____

_____

_____

_____

6 A third reminder

Read the third reminder from Ms. Valdez.

> Dear Mr. Piaget:
>
> This is the third reminder I have sent about invoice #3204 (copy enclosed). The invoice is now four months overdue.
>
> If we do not receive payment within five business days, we will have no choice but to take legal action.
>
> We look forward to receiving payment immediately.
>
> Sincerely yours,
>
> *Anita Valdez*
>
> Anita Valdez

Circle the correct word for each sentence.

a Ms. Valdez has sent two / three previous letters to Mr. Piaget.
b She has been waiting for payment for three / four months.
c The letter is polite / impolite.
d Ms. Valdez is joking / serious about taking legal action.

7 Using the conditional

1 Underline the first conditional sentence in the previous letter. (It begins with *if*.)

2

The *if* clause describes a situation that may or may not happen in the future. The other (main) clause tells us the result. Together the two clauses make a conditional sentence. **Note:** Do not use *will* in the *if* clause.

SITUATION	RESULT
If we do not receive payment within five business days,	we will take legal action.

Write conditional sentences using the ideas below. Use a different time period in the *if* clause each time.

EXAMPLE contact a collection agency
If we do not receive payment within two weeks, we will contact a collection agency.

a stop doing business with you

_____

b review our relationship with your company

_____

c insist on payment in advance for all future business

_____

d terminate our agreement with your company

_____

8 Writing task 2 **1** Work with a new partner. You both work for the same company. You are waiting for a customer to pay a bill. Invent information for each heading below and write it on a separate piece of paper.

Name of contact:

Invoice number:

Type of product / service:

Date due:

2 Exchange this information with another pair of students. Now write a reminder letter to the customer using the information you have received. It can be a first, second, or third reminder.

10 Complaints

1 A complaint and a response

1 Read the emails.

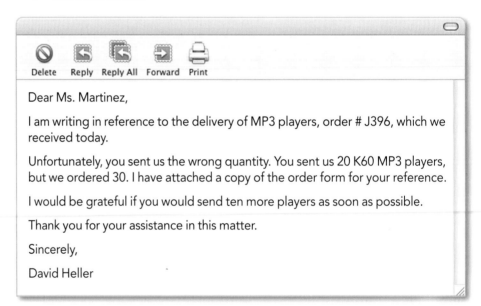

Dear Ms. Martinez,

I am writing in reference to the delivery of MP3 players, order # J396, which we received today.

Unfortunately, you sent us the wrong quantity. You sent us 20 K60 MP3 players, but we ordered 30. I have attached a copy of the order form for your reference.

I would be grateful if you would send ten more players as soon as possible.

Thank you for your assistance in this matter.

Sincerely,

David Heller

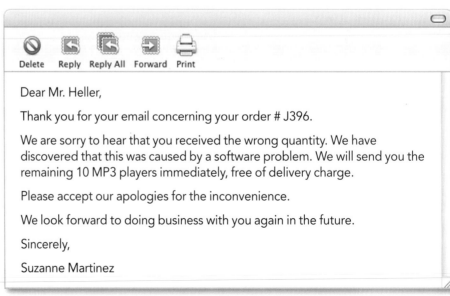

Dear Mr. Heller,

Thank you for your email concerning your order # J396.

We are sorry to hear that you received the wrong quantity. We have discovered that this was caused by a software problem. We will send you the remaining 10 MP3 players immediately, free of delivery charge.

Please accept our apologies for the inconvenience.

We look forward to doing business with you again in the future.

Sincerely,

Suzanne Martinez

2   Answer the questions.

a   Which order is David Heller writing about?

_____

b   What is the problem?

_____

c   What is Mr. Heller sending with the email?

_____

d   What does Mr. Heller want Ms. Martinez to do?

_____

e   What reason does Ms. Martinez give for the problem?

_____

f   When will Ms. Martinez's company send the other MP3 players?

_____

g   Does Mr. Heller's company have to pay for the shipment?

_____

2 Introducing the topic   1

TIP!

When you write a complaint letter, fax, or email:
— send the complaint as soon as possible
— explain the situation clearly
— suggest a way of solving the problem
— be polite
— don't apologize for complaining

LANGUAGE FOCUS

You can use these expressions to begin your message:

I am writing to complain about …
I am writing about a problem with …
I am writing in reference to …

Note: The first two sentences have a stronger complaining tone than the third.

Write sentences using the expressions above and the phrases below. Use each expression at least once.

EXAMPLE order # 7214-649
I am writing to complain about order # 7214-649.

a   your latest shipment

_____

b   the installation of computer network software

_____

c   order # XJ 4311

_____

d   the redecoration of our corporate headquarters

_____

2 LANGUAGE FOCUS

You can add extra information about a topic, like this:

I am writing to complain about order # 7214-649.
(extra information) It arrived yesterday.

I am writing to complain about order # 7212-649, which arrived yesterday.

Add extra information and combine the sentences in exercise 2.1 in the same way.

a   It was delivered this morning.

_____

b   It was completed last week.

_____

c   It arrived on Friday.

_____

d   It was finished yesterday.

_____

3 Explaining the situation

LANGUAGE FOCUS

First, say what the problem is:

We regret to inform you that	the goods were damaged.
I am sorry to say that	the shipment arrived late.
Unfortunately,	you sent us the wrong model.
	the work was unsatisfactory.

Then give details:

We ordered TS400 models, but we received TS300.
There are cracks in the walls.
The plastic casings were scratched in several places.
The promised delivery date was January 22, but it arrived February 6.

If necessary, add any further information:

We enclose	a copy	of the	order.
Please find enclosed	a photocopy		shipping order.
I am attaching	photographs		damage.
			work.

We can combine the sentences above like this:

EXAMPLE   *I am sorry to say that the goods were damaged. The plastic casings were scratched in several places. We enclose photographs of the damage.*

Match the three other sentences in the same way.

a   _____

_____

_____

66   Writing for the Real World

b _____

c _____

4 Suggesting a solution

1 Fill in the blanks, using the words below.

inspect   items   ensure   replacement

a Please send us the correct _____ by January 14.
b Please _____ that future shipments arrive on time.
c Please send us the _____ goods as soon as possible.
d Please send someone to _____ the building immediately.

2 Talk to a partner. Match the solutions above to the situations in exercise 3.

5 Writing task 1

Write a complaint email. You can use the email in exercise 1.1 as a model. Use your own ideas or the ideas below.

6 Responding to a complaint

1 Look at this advice for responding to a complaint. Fill in the blanks, using the words below.

give   write   thank   refer   say

a _____ your customer for writing to you.

b _____ to the problem and apologize.

c _____ an explanation for the problem, if possible.

d _____ how you are going to help the customer.

e _____ a polite conclusion.

2 The sentences below are from a letter responding to a complaint. Number them in the correct order.

Dear Mr. Watanabe,

☐ We will send you the correct items free of delivery charge.

☐ We are sorry to hear that you received the wrong order.

☐ Once again, please accept our apologies for the inconvenience, and we look forward to serving you again in the future.

☐ Thank you for your letter dated October 26 concerning your recent order.

☐ Apparently, this was caused by a processing error.

Sincerely,

Vince Picardo

Vince Picardo

3 Write the phrases in the letter opposite which have the same meaning as these items.

a regarding   _____

b we regret to learn   _____

c this was the result of   _____

d at no extra cost   _____

e we apologize   _____

4 Rewrite the letter in exercise 6.2, using the expressions in exercise 6.3 and this information.

- Ms. Pang
- email / May 10 / the installation of computer accounting software
- the installation was unsatisfactory
- was caused by a fault in the CD
- will send a replacement CD immediately

7 Writing task 2

1 Find a partner. Exchange the letters of complaint you wrote in exercise 5.

2 Write a response to your partner's letter of complaint, using your own ideas. You can use the letter in exercise 6.2 as a model.

Review 2

1 Placing and responding to an order

1 Complete the email. Choose the correct prepositions from the box.

for   by   of   within   to   on   of

To: Joe Abbott

Cc:

Subject: Urgent order

Dear Mr. Abbott,

Following our conversation [1] _____ the telephone this morning, I would like to place an order [2] _____ the following art supplies:

QUANTITY	DESCRIPTION	CODE	UNIT PRICE
15	PK System drawing boards	ES1712	$58.94
50 packs	Drawing paper	RS1441	$18.12
20 boxes	Classicolor pencils	JA1043	$7.73
10 packs	Water color brush set	DL956	$7.87

As we agreed:

– you will send the goods [3] _____ express delivery
– the goods will be sent [4] _____ five working days [5] _____ receipt of this order
– I will receive a discount [6] _____ 10%
– you will charge the amount [7] _____ my account, number 079-100457

I look forward to receiving your acknowledgment.

With best wishes,

Anton van Hoek

---

2 Use the following notes to write a reply to Mr. van Hoek's email. Look at Unit 8 if you need more help.
— acknowledge Mr. van Hoek's email
— explain that one item, the PK System drawing board, is out of stock – apologize
— suggest an alternative – the Contura drawing board – similar price and quality – details on website / page 10 of catalog
— confirm the shipping details

Remember to include a salutation at the beginning of your email and a complimentary closing at the end.

2 Word puzzle

Write the answers to the clues below in the puzzle. When you have finished, read down to find the answer to this question:

What do you call a company that sells goods to the general public?

a *At no extra cost* means the same as "f_____ of charge".

b If you want to find out more about a company's products or services, you can write to them and make i_____.

c "To c_____" means the same as *to finish*.

d Another word for *buy* is "p_____".

e A c_____ of hotels is a group of hotels owned by the same company.

f An e_____ is a person who works for a company in return for a salary.

g When you respond to a complaint, you should apologize and suggest a way to s_____ the problem.

h A f_____ is a place where goods are manufactured.

3 Pairwork dictation

1 Work with a partner. Take turns reading sentences to your partner, who will write them down.
Student A: Use the sentences on page 109.
Student B: Use the sentences on page 110.

> **LANGUAGE FOCUS**
>
> Could you say that again?
> Could you speak more slowly?
> How do you spell "…"?
> What's the (fourth) word?

Now write the sentences that your partner reads out to you.

a _____
b _____
c _____
d _____
e _____
f _____

2 When you have finished, compare your sentences with your partner's page. Did you spell everything correctly?

4 Correct the mistakes

Below is the first draft of an email message replying to a complaint. There are two mistakes in each of the following:

— spelling
— punctuation
— capitalization
— verb tenses
— prepositions

Find the ten mistakes and correct them.

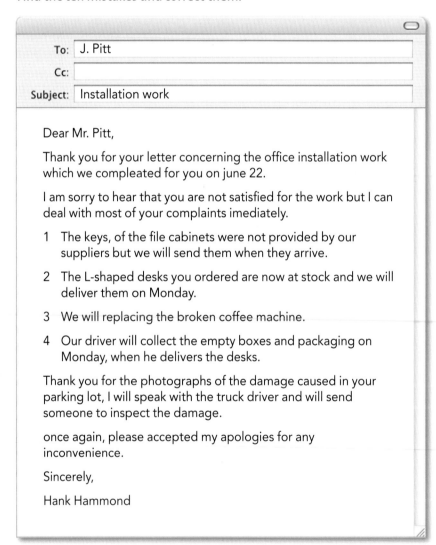

To: J. Pitt

Cc:

Subject: Installation work

Dear Mr. Pitt,

Thank you for your letter concerning the office installation work which we compleated for you on june 22.

I am sorry to hear that you are not satisfied for the work but I can deal with most of your complaints imediately.

1 The keys, of the file cabinets were not provided by our suppliers but we will send them when they arrive.

2 The L-shaped desks you ordered are now at stock and we will deliver them on Monday.

3 We will replacing the broken coffee machine.

4 Our driver will collect the empty boxes and packaging on Monday, when he delivers the desks.

Thank you for the photographs of the damage caused in your parking lot, I will speak with the truck driver and will send someone to inspect the damage.

once again, please accepted my apologies for any inconvenience.

Sincerely,

Hank Hammond

5 Reminders about late payment

1 Read the letters and answer the questions below. Write short answers.

Dear Ms. Figo,

Thank you for the shipment of 500 teapots which we received yesterday.

We are pleased to inform you that we have instructed our bank to transfer €3,254.00 to your account in payment of invoice number PI/017. Could you please notify us that the transfer has been made?

I look forward to hearing from you.

Sincerely yours,

Juan Pires

Juan Pires

Dear Mr. Pires,

This is the second reminder I have sent you about invoice number PI/017. On April 5 I wrote to inform you that the transfer of €3,254.00 to our bank account did not take place. I have not received a reply to my letter and the invoice is now three months overdue.

I look forward to receiving payment at your earliest convenience.

Sincerely yours,

Anne-Marie Figo

Anne-Marie Figo

---

a What was in the shipment from Ms. Figo to Mr. Pires?
b How much did the shipment cost?
c How will Mr. Pires pay for the shipment?
d Did the bank transfer take place?
e Is this Ms. Figo's first reminder letter?
f How late is the payment?
g What does Ms. Figo want Mr. Pires to do next?
h What does *at your earliest convenience* mean?

2 Ms. Figo asked her assistant to write to Mr. Pires again. Use the notes below to write the letter. Look at Unit 9 if you need more help.

Please write third reminder to Mr Pires – please pay within 10 days – if not, please pay in advance in future

11 Checking progress

IN THIS UNIT, YOU WILL LEARN HOW TO ...

▶ check progress on a task or project

▶ explain progress on a task or project

▶ write about cause and effect

▶ use the present perfect tense

---

1 Two inquiries

1 Erika Mitchell is the editor of ABC Corporation's house newsletter. She often commissions illustrations from Stefan Forbes and photographs from Yumiko Naganuma. Read the email extracts. Write the correct letter (A–D) on the lines below. Which email is ...

1 Erika's inquiry to Stefan? _____
2 Stefan's reply to Erika? _____
3 Erika's inquiry to Yumiko? _____
4 Yumiko's reply to Erika? _____

A

Delete Reply Reply All Forward Print

Everything's going well. I've finished the exterior shots, but I haven't done the interiors yet. I'll finish them this week and send you the complete batch by Friday.

B

Delete Reply Reply All Forward Print

Thanks for your email. I had a problem with my computer. It crashed and I lost some data. As a result, I had to redo some of the illustrations. Will Friday be all right? Apologies for the delay.

C

Delete Reply Reply All Forward Print

How are the photographs going? I'm looking forward to seeing them.

D

Delete Reply Reply All Forward Print

According to the schedule we agreed on last month, the illustrations for this month's issue were due yesterday. Are they ready yet?

2 Are these statements about the emails true (T) or false (F)? Check (✓) the correct box.

		T	F
a	The illustrations were due yesterday.	☐	☐
b	The illustrations are ready now.	☐	☐
c	Stefan had a problem with his computer.	☐	☐
d	Erika doesn't want to see the photographs.	☐	☐
e	Yumiko is behind schedule.	☐	☐
f	Yumiko will send all the photographs by Friday.	☐	☐

2 Checking progress

LANGUAGE FOCUS

☺ **If you want to check progress on a task, you can ask:**

How is the report going?
How are you getting along with the report?
Is the report going well?

☺ **If you are a little worried about progress, you can use:**

I'm	a little	worried	about the report.
	somewhat	concerned	

Is everything	OK?
	all right?
	on schedule?

☹ **If you are worried about progress, use more formal language:**

According to my	schedule, notes,	the report	was due yesterday. is overdue.
		the deadline the completion date	for the report was yesterday.
Please let me know if		you are having any problems. there is a problem.	

Use the above expressions to write about the tasks suggested in a–e. Use a different expression each time.

a the preparations for the trade fair ☺

_____

b the software installation ☺

_____

c the new website design ☹

_____

d the market research ☺

_____

e next year's sales forecast ☹

_____

LANGUAGE FOCUS

You can answer questions about progress on a task like this:

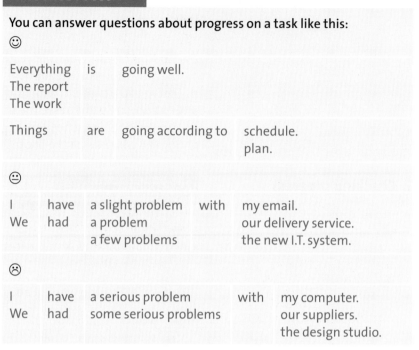

☺

Everything The report The work	is	going well.	
Things	are	going according to	schedule. plan.

☺

I We	have had	a slight problem a problem a few problems	with	my email. our delivery service. the new I.T. system.

☹

I We	have had	a serious problem some serious problems	with	my computer. our suppliers. the design studio.

Use the above expressions to write answers about the situations in exercise 2. Use a different expression each time. You can use the present continuous, simple present, or simple past tense.

a the preparations for the trade fair ☺
   we / slight problem / the booth equipment

b the software installation ☹
   we / some serious problems / the old computers

c the new website design ☺
   everything / plan

d the market research ☺
   I / slight problem / the questionnaire results

e next year's sales forecast ☺
   things / schedule

4 Cause and effect

When we explain a problem, we often mention the cause and the effect. You can use *as a result*, *so*, and *consequently* to link the cause to the effect:

CAUSE			EFFECT
My alarm clock didn't go off	.	As a result, Consequently,	I had to rush to get ready.
		, so	

George Thomson went on a business trip to Chicago. Write four cause and effect sentences about his trip, using this information. Use each expression above at least once.

EXAMPLE   My alarm clock didn't go off. As a result, I had to rush to get ready.

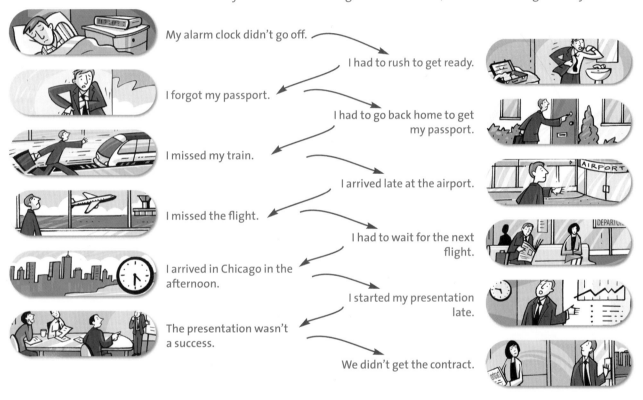

My alarm clock didn't go off.

I had to rush to get ready.

I forgot my passport.

I had to go back home to get my passport.

I missed my train.

I arrived late at the airport.

I missed the flight.

I had to wait for the next flight.

I arrived in Chicago in the afternoon.

I started my presentation late.

The presentation wasn't a success.

We didn't get the contract.

I had to rush to get ready, so I forgot my passport. I forgot my passport, so …

_____

_____

_____

_____

_____

5 Completed and uncompleted tasks

You can use the present perfect tense to ask and answer about completed and uncompleted tasks like this:

COMPLETED TASK

(contact Mr. Ali?   ✓ – this morning)
Have you contacted Mr. Ali (yet)?
(Yes,) I've contacted Mr. Ali. I did it this morning.

UNCOMPLETED TASK

(order the new software?   ✗ – as soon as possible)
Have you ordered the new software (yet)?
(No,) I haven't ordered the new software yet. I'll do it as soon as possible.

Write similar questions and responses for each item below.

a   make a reservation at L'Epinade   ✓ – yesterday

_____

_____

_____

_____

b   reserve a meeting room   ✗ – this afternoon

_____

_____

_____

_____

c   prepare an information pack   ✗ – today

_____

_____

_____

_____

d   send out invitations   ✓ – this morning

_____

_____

_____

_____

6 Writing task 1

Work with a partner. Choose one of the situations below and write an email inquiring about progress. In each case you can use given names and an informal writing style.

Situation 1

Your company:	Apex Electonics
Your position:	Marketing manager
Project:	The Apex stand at the Electronics Trade Fair
Your task:	Write an email to Elaine Chung in the publicity department. She is organizing the delivery of equipment for the booth.
Comment:	You are not worried about progress – you just want to check.

Situation 2

Your company:	Murata Securities
Your position:	I.T. manager
Project:	Installation of new back-up hardware and software in the New York branch
Your task:	Write an email to Helmut Frick, the I.T. manager. He is in charge of the installation.
Comment:	You are a little worried about progress.

Situation 3

Your company:	Cafferty's Confectionery
Your position:	Sales manager
Project:	Market research on taste preferences among teenage consumers
Your task:	Write an email to Lisa Ingram in the product development department. She is in charge of the project.
Comment:	You are very worried about progress.

7 Writing task 2

1 Find another pair of students and exchange the emails you wrote in exercise 6. You are going to write one of the replies below. Toss a coin to decide which reply to write. Heads = Reply A; tails = Reply B.

TIP!

You can apologize (informally and politely) like this:
I'm sorry for the delay.
Sorry for the inconvenience.

2 With your partner, make notes for your reply, then write the email.

Reply A
— Thank the writer for his / her email.
— Say what your problem is / was.
— Say what the cause and effect is / was.
— Say when you can complete the task.
— If necessary, apologize.

Reply B
— Thank the writer for his / her email.
— Say that everything is going according to schedule.
— Say one thing you have done.
— Say one thing you haven't done.
— Say when you can complete the task.

12 Interoffice memos

IN THIS UNIT YOU WILL LEARN HOW TO ...

▶ write a short memo

▶ announce recent events

▶ announce future events

▶ make formal requests

1 Three memos

1 Read the memos and write the correct subject on the subject line of each memo. Choose from these subjects:

a Company health club
b New general manager
c New sales manager

d Closure of cafeteria
e Meeting postponed
f Conference rooms

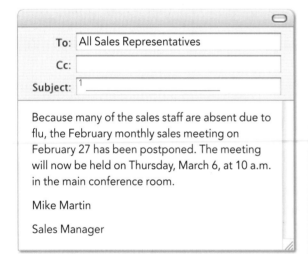

To: All Sales Representatives
Cc:
Subject: 1 _____

Because many of the sales staff are absent due to flu, the February monthly sales meeting on February 27 has been postponed. The meeting will now be held on Thursday, March 6, at 10 a.m. in the main conference room.

Mike Martin

Sales Manager

Fujisaki Optics Ltd.

MEMO

Date: January 17, 2006
To: All staff
From: Bill Dawes
Subject: 2 _____

Karen Walker has been appointed general manager following the retirement of Brent Larsen. All staff are requested to attend an informal meeting in the cafeteria Monday January 21 at 4:30 p.m. where they will be introduced to Ms. Walker.

MT Communications Inc.   **MEMO**

Date: February 4, 2006
To: All employees
From: Alice Goto
Subject: 3 _____

The new company health club has been completed and will be open from Monday, February 9. Opening hours will be 7:00 – 9:00 a.m. and 5:30 – 9:30 p.m. Monday to Friday.

If you would like to use the health club, please fill out the attached registration form.

2 Write short answers to the questions. Then check your answers with a partner.

a Who is the new general manager?

_____

b When can the staff meet her?

_____

c Which meeting has been postponed?

_____

d Why has it been postponed?

_____

e What has just been completed?

_____

f How many days a week will the company health club be open?

_____

2 Writing a memo

1 Work with a partner. Are these statements about memos true (T) or false (F)?

	T	F
a *Memo* is short for *memorandum*.	☐	☐
b A memo is usually sent to more than one person.	☐	☐
c A memo is usually sent to people in a different company.	☐	☐
d You should always reply to a memo.	☐	☐
e You can write a memo on paper or as an email.	☐	☐

2 Fill in the blanks in the paper memo below using this information:

August 21   Grinder Guitars, Inc.   All employees   Thefts
Dan Ellis   there have been a number of thefts in the building recently

1 _____

Memo _____

DATE: 2 _____
TO: 3 _____
FROM: 4 _____
SUBJECT: 5 _____

As you know, 6 _____ .
All employees are reminded to keep their personal
belongings safe at all times and use the lockers provided.

▶ See page 117 for more information on memos.

3 Writing about recent events

LANGUAGE FOCUS

To announce a recent event, you can use the simple past tense and a time expression:
We *interviewed* six applicants for the position of I.T. manager last week.

If the time when something happened (e.g., last week) is not important, or you don't want to mention it, you can use the present perfect without a time expression:
We *have interviewed* six applicants for the position of production manager.

You can change a passive sentence in the same way:
The new cafeteria *was completed* on March 16.
The new cafeteria *has been completed*.

Rewrite these sentences using the present perfect without a time expression.

a Jean Perrier from the Paris office was appointed manager of the New York office last week.

_____

b The June monthly sales meeting was postponed this morning.

_____

c Last week we decided to increase the sales staff.

_____

d New cycling and running machines were ordered at the end of last month.

_____

2 Work with a partner. Write three sentences like the ones you wrote in exercise 3.1, using the passive voice and present perfect tense. Use the ideas below.

a new computers (install)

b the new library (complete)

c new "No Smoking" policy (introduce)

a _____
b _____
c _____

4 Announcing events in the future

1

You can use *will* with the passive to announce events in the future:

The Christmas party *will be held* on December 23.
The new model *will be introduced* next month.

Complete the sentences below using the correct form of the verb in brackets.

a   The positions _____ next month. (advertise)

b   He _____ as manager of the Paris office by Paul Kraus. (succeed)

c   The new equipment _____ by the end of this month. (install)

d   The next meeting _____ on July 7 at the usual time. (hold)

2   Match the sentences in exercise 3.1 with the ones in exercise 4.1. Write one matching pair of sentences below.

EXAMPLE   *Jean Perrier has been appointed manager of the New York office.*

He will be succeeded as manager of the Paris office by Paul Kraus.

_____

_____

_____

3   Write a second sentence using *will* and the passive for each sentence you wrote in exercise 3.2. Use your own ideas or the ideas below.

a   orientation session / hold / 9 a.m. / Monday, September 6

_____

_____

b   books, magazines, and CD-ROMs / be available

_____

_____

c   be enforced with immediate effect

_____

_____

5 Formal requests

You can write a strong, but polite request like this:

All sales staff are requested to attend the meeting.

Would all sales staff please attend the meeting.

Please contact the personnel department for more details.

Rewrite the words of the sentences in the correct order. Pay attention to capital letters and punctuation.

a   are requested / the enclosed form / to complete / all employees

_____

b   their computers / would / turn off / before leaving / all staff

_____

c   me / any questions / please / with / email

_____

6 An email memo

Memos are often sent as emails. Fill in the blanks in the email memo. Use the words below.

will   about   or   is   on   been   Please

To: All staff

Cc: Susan Westgate

Subject: New Website Design

As you know, our website has 1 _____ redesigned and a beta version 2 _____ now available 3 _____ the company intranet. The newly-designed website 4 _____ be launched on August 1. 5 _____ email any comments or suggestions 6 _____ the website to me 7 _____ Larry Topaz in Online Marketing.

Susan

7 Writing task 1

Work with a partner. Write an email memo from Debra Pavlov, manager of the Human Resources Department. Use these notes:

- Mr. Ken Oda of Pacific Enterprises
- visit our corporate headquarters and factory May 5-7
- Peter Hare will show him around
- be ready to answer Mr. Oda's questions

From:	
Date:	
To:	
Subject:	

8 Writing task 2

With your partner, write a paper or email memo about a real or imaginary event or situation at your company or school.

promote to / Human Resources Manager

open / new language center

not eat / at your desk

have / important visitor to factory

receive / Employee of the Year award

13 Discussing proposals

1 The annual sales conference

1 Mark Chung is the international sales manager of an electronics company based in Singapore. He sent the email below to the regional sales managers in other countries. Read the email and answer the questions.

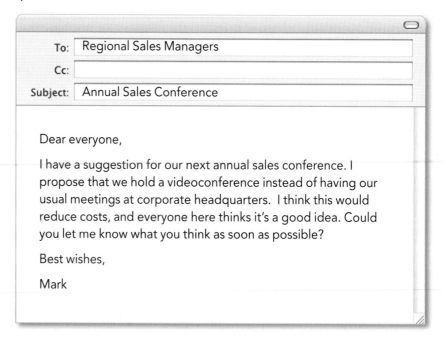

To: Regional Sales Managers

Cc:

Subject: Annual Sales Conference

Dear everyone,

I have a suggestion for our next annual sales conference. I propose that we hold a videoconference instead of having our usual meetings at corporate headquarters. I think this would reduce costs, and everyone here thinks it's a good idea. Could you let me know what you think as soon as possible?

Best wishes,

Mark

a What is the email about?

_____

b What does he suggest?

_____

c What reason does he give for his suggestion?

_____

d When does he want to know everyone's opinion?

_____

2 Read four replies to Mark's email and write the name of the correct person (Kazuo, Marianne, Bill, or Amy) to complete each sentence below.

a _____ agrees with Mark's suggestion.

b _____ disagrees with Mark's suggestion and gives a reason.

c _____ disagrees with Mark's suggestion and proposes another idea.

d _____ is uncertain about Mark's suggestion.

Delete Reply Reply All Forward Print

Sorry, but I don't think a videoconference is a very good idea. In my opinion, face-to-face contact is very important.

Best wishes,
Kazuo

Delete Reply Reply All Forward Print

To be honest, I don't like the idea of having a videoconference. But what about meeting at a conference center in Tahiti instead of at corporate headquarters?

Marianne

Delete Reply Reply All Forward Print

I'm not sure about your idea of holding a videoconference. Can I get back to you later today? Cheers,

Bill

Delete Reply Reply All Forward Print

I think holding a videoconference is a great idea. Is it expensive to set up?

Regards,
Amy

2 Making a proposal

You can use these expressions to introduce a proposal:

I have	a proposal an idea a suggestion	for our next annual sales conference.

You can use these expressions to make a proposal:

How What	about	holding a videoconference?
I think we should I propose that we		hold a videoconference.

Write about the ideas below using the language above. Use each expression at least once.

EXAMPLE the meeting tomorrow / start with a brainstorming session

I have a proposal for the meeting tomorrow. How about starting with a brainstorming session?

a the new office layout / make the reception area smaller

_____

_____

b the summer sale / sell everything at one price

_____

_____

c the staff party / hire a rap group

_____

_____

d the cafeteria / just serve sandwiches and salads

_____

_____

e Jeff's retirement gift / give him a set of golf clubs

_____

_____

3 Giving a reason

When you make a proposal, you usually give a reason:

I propose that we hold a videoconference.

I think	it	would reduce costs.
For one thing,	this	
One reason is that		more people could participate.

Match each proposal with the correct reason. Then write complete sentences.

a	upgrade our presentation hardware	1	brighten the place up
b	find a bigger meeting room	2	make presentations more effective
c	hold the international sales meeting twice a year	3	improve security
d	put more art on the walls	4	help us respond to the markets faster
e	introduce CCTV cameras	5	more people could attend

a *How about upgrading our presentation software? For one thing, it would make presentations more effective.*

b _____

_____

c _____

_____

d _____

_____

e _____

_____

4 Reporting other people's opinions

To report opinions you can use the simple present tense:
John: "I think it's a good idea."
John thinks it's a good idea.

Fill in the blanks using the correct form of the verb in parentheses.

a Jane _____ it's an excellent idea. (think)
b Angela and Pierre _____ with the proposal. (agree)
c Everyone at corporate headquarters _____ the idea. (like)
d The design staff _____ it's an interesting proposal. (think)
e Everyone here _____ in favor of the proposal. (be)

5 Asking for an opinion

LANGUAGE FOCUS

To ask for an opinion, you can use:

| Could you let me | know what you think | as soon as possible? |
| | have | your opinion
any comments | by Friday?
before our next meeting? |

Rewrite the sentences below in the correct order. Pay attention to capital letters and punctuation.

a could / the meeting tomorrow / let me have / before / your opinion / you

_____

b you / what / could / as soon as possible / let me know / you think

_____

c by / you / could / any comments / next Monday / let me have

_____

_____

6 Giving your opinion

LANGUAGE FOCUS

Giving a favorable opinion:

| I think | it's | an excellent | idea. |
| In my opinion, | | a very good | proposal. |

Expressing uncertainty:

| I'm not sure. | | Can I get back to you? |
| I'm not sure about | the idea.
your proposal. | |

Giving an unfavorable opinion:

I don't think it's a (very) good idea.
In my opinion, it's not a (very) good idea.

Respond to the proposals in exercise 2. Use a different expression each time.

+   = giving a favorable opinion
+ / −   = expressing uncertainty
−   = giving an unfavorable opinion

EXAMPLE *(+ / −) I'm not sure about the idea. Can I get back to you?*

a (−) _____
b (+) _____
c (+ / −) _____
d (+) _____

TIP!

If you are not ready to give an opinion, you can use:
It sounds interesting, but can I think about it?

7 Suggesting an alternative

LANGUAGE FOCUS

When you don't agree with a proposal, you can use these three stages:

(Proposal):

I think we should move our headquarters to the suburbs.

— **Say you don't agree:** I don't think it's a good idea.

— **Give a reason:**

| I think | it will be inconvenient for many employees. |
| For one thing, | |

— **Suggest an alternative:**

| I think | we should | stay in the downtown area. |
| | it would be better to | |

Using your own ideas, write responses for the proposals. Write three sentences for each response, following the stages in the *Language focus* box above.

EXAMPLE make the office reception area smaller

I don't think it's a good idea. It would give a bad impression. I think we should make it as large as possible.

a hire a rap group for the staff party

_____

b give Jeff a set of golf clubs for his retirement gift

_____

c put more art on the office walls

_____

8 Writing task

1 Work in pairs. Imagine that you both work for X Corporation (think of a name). Each student should choose a different topic from the three below.

— You want to cut your company's production costs.
— You want to increase your company's brand recognition.
— You want to improve employee morale.

2 Now work alone. Think of a proposal for your topic and write an email to your partner. You can use Mark's email in exercise 1 as a model.

— Introduce your proposal.
— Make your proposal.
— Report the favorable opinion(s) of your colleague(s).
— Ask for an opinion.
— Say when you want to receive a response.

3 Exchange emails with your partner and write a response. You can agree or disagree with your colleague's proposal, or say that you are unsure. Give a reason for your opinion. If you disagree, suggest an alternative.

14 Reports

1 A report

1 Jack Vasari works for Larsen, an American ice cream company. Read his report. Is the main topic:

a a business trip? b a new market? c a new product?

JAPAN REPORT

Introduction

Earlier this month, I visited Japan to investigate the possibility of introducing our products there. Although Larsen is a leading ice cream producer in the United States, it is not well known in Japan.

The Market

The ice cream market in Japan is very competitive, and is now open to foreign companies. Sales of regular and high-quality products have risen steadily in recent years (see attached sales figures). I visited wholesalers, retailers, and sales reps in the Tokyo and Osaka areas, and also spoke to consumer focus groups. I discovered that Japanese consumers pay attention to:

a) flavor: lighter flavors are popular

b) image: effective advertising and attractive packaging are essential

c) ingredients: all ingredients must be pure and information should be provided on packaging

d) package / portion size: sizes are generally much smaller than in the U.S.

e) price: although we are not aiming for the lower-end market, prices should be no higher than those of our main competitors

f) etiquette: outside the home, Japanese consumers prefer to eat ice cream at the point of purchase; eating in the street is generally not acceptable, although this is changing.

Conclusion

Based on my research, I suggest that we first introduce a limited range of U.S.-made lines in retail stores. We should immediately investigate the possibility of production in Japan, and I recommend that we offer a number of ice cream café franchises in the Tokyo area as soon as possible.

2 Write short answers to the questions.

a   Is Larsen well-known in Japan? _____

b   Where did Jack go in Japan? _____

c   Is the Japanese market growing? _____

d   Are consumers only interested in flavor? _____

e   Does Jack think Larsen should sell ice cream in Japan? _____

2 Report layout

A report usually follows this sequence:

Title:	a short, clear explanation of what the report is about
Introduction:	a summary of the report
Main body:	the important facts
Conclusion:	the writer's opinions based on the facts in the body of the report

Read the sentences below. They are from two different reports. Which reports are they from? Write "1" or "2" beside each item. Then, next to each one write "T" (Title), "I" (Introduction), "B" (Body), or "C" (Conclusion).

_____ I recommend that we continue the program, and encourage other hotels to do the same.

_____ We found that the program cut laundry costs by up to 24% and improved our image among guests.

_1T_ _ _ _ *Linen Reuse Program: a Progress Report*

_____ I have now completed my inquiry into the poor sales of the V602 camcorder.

_____ *The Future of the V602 Camcorder*

_____ I present below an overview of the linen reuse program. Further details can be found in the attachment.

_____ Based on my research, I strongly suggest that we replace the V602 model.

_____ I found that 90% of consumers in our survey think that the V602 model is too large and too heavy.

3 Vocabulary

We often use more formal vocabulary when we write a report. Match the more formal verbs and verb phrases (a–i) with the less formal expressions (1–9).

a   go to (a place)

b   ask someone questions

c   go from place to place

d   find out about

e   talk about

f   give

g   start selling a product

h   have meetings with someone

i   go to (a meeting / conference)

1   tour

2   visit

3   introduce a product

4   attend

5   hold discussions with someone

6   investigate

7   provide

8   interview

9   discuss

4 Giving a reason

1

Look at these two sentences:

Earlier this month, I visited Italy.

The reason for my trip was to investigate the possibility of introducing our products there.

You can combine them like this:

Earlier this month, I visited Italy to investigate the possibility of introducing our products there.

Write sentences using the information below.

EXAMPLE   last month / visit Seoul / attend the international Plastics Show
Last month, I visited Seoul to attend the International Plastics Show.

a   at the end of last month / fly to Taiwan / visit the new Taipei plant

_____

b   earlier this month / go to Germany / hold discussions with our subsidiary in Karlsruhe

_____

c   two weeks ago / fly to Toronto / investigate the Canadian market

_____

d   last week / visit Chicago / discuss the new office with Ichiro Sato

_____
_____

2   Write a similar sentence (real or imaginary) about yourself.

_____
_____
_____

5 Describing charts and graphs

Look at these two bar charts:

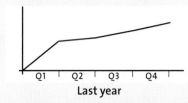 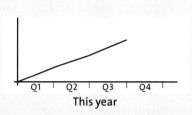

Last year	This year

In the first quarter, sales rose sharply.
So far this year, sales have risen sharply.

To write about a finished time period, use the simple past:

Last year, During the second / third / final quarter, Last July,	sales profits costs production consumption	rose slightly / sharply. remained constant. fell slightly / sharply.

To write about an unfinished time period, use the present perfect:

So far this year, During the past five years, Recently,	sales profits costs	have	risen slightly / sharply. remained constant. fallen slightly / sharply.
	production consumption	has	

Write about the information below, using the simple past or present perfect.

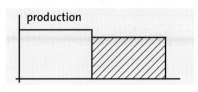 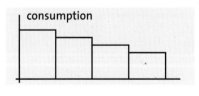 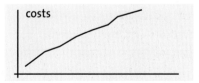 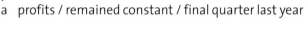

a profits / remained constant / final quarter last year

_____

_____

b consumption / has fallen slightly / past two years

_____

_____

c costs / risen sharply / so far this year

_____

_____

d production / fell slightly / last year

_____

_____

6 Analyzing a market

1

You can write about consumer preferences like this:

I discovered that	most	customers	are concerned about …
I found that	the majority of	consumers	are worried about …
According to my research,		users	are interested in …
			pay attention to …

Write about the markets below, using one or two of the ideas below in each sentence. You can use your own ideas, too.

price	quality	health issues	taste
ease of use	operating costs	attractive design	location
atmosphere	security	safety	

EXAMPLE automobiles
I discovered that most consumers are interested in safety and running costs.

a housing

_____

_____

b DVD recorders

_____

_____

c coffee shops

_____

_____

d Internet banking

_____

_____

e cosmetics

_____

_____

2 Discuss your ideas with a partner.

3 Write a similar sentence (real or imaginary) about your company's customers or your school's students.

_____

_____

7 Making recommendations

LANGUAGE FOCUS

You can recommend action like this:

Based on	my research, the research outlined above, the information above,	I recommend (that) we I suggest (that) we I think (that) we should	first introduce a limited range of products.

Write the words in the sentences in the correct order. Pay attention to capitalization and punctuation.

a   the VX371 model / outlined above / the research / stop production of / I think that / based on / we should

_____

_____

b   models / I recommend that / the prices of / based on / our top of the line / we reduce / the information above

_____

_____

c   we outsource / to New Delhi / my research / I suggest that / based on / our customer support services

_____

_____

8 Writing task

REMEMBER!

When you write a report, include:
— a title
— an introduction
— the body of the report
— a conclusion (with recommendations, if necessary)

Write a report about a real or imaginary business trip you have made. Use Jack's report in exercise 1 as a model. If you prefer, you can use this situation:

Your company:	Kanto Timber Co. Ltd. (Japan)
You went to:	Canada
When:	last month
Why:	to speak to Canadian timber suppliers
You discovered:	quality is excellent, but prices are high
Recommendations:	need to negotiate price and discounts

15 Social situations

▶ write to congratulate

▶ express sympathy and condolences

▶ write to thank

▶ use a letter, email, or greeting card as appropriate

1 Six situations

1 Read the six extracts from correspondence to colleagues and business acquaintances and write the correct letter (a–f) next to each one.

a a letter thanking a speaker for a presentation to a business association

b an email congratulating a colleague on her promotion

c a letter to a colleague expressing sympathy about an accident

d an email to a colleague who is retiring

e a message on a condolence card to the wife of a business acquaintance

f a message on a seasonal greeting card to a business acquaintance

1 ☐ We hope you'll make a speedy recovery, and hope to see you soon.

2 ☐ We were shocked to hear of Tetsuo's sudden death. We had the greatest respect for him and know that he will be greatly missed by everyone.

3 ☐ I am sure that you will be a great success in your new position. Let's stay in touch.

4 ☐ Martina and I hope you are all well. We send our good wishes for the new year!

5 ☐ Everyone found the evening enjoyable and inspiring, and we hope that you will be able to address our group again next year.

6 ☐ I am sure you are looking forward to having more time to play golf. I know that we are all going to miss you.

2 Write the words and phrases in the extracts above which have the same or similar meanings to the items below:

a quick _____

b unexpected _____

c job _____

d in good health _____

e speak to _____

f certain _____

2 Congratulating

TIP!

You can congratulate a business acquaintance on a business-related event by letter, or less formally, by email. A handwritten letter adds a personal touch. For social events, such as a marriage or birth, you can send a greeting card with a short handwritten message. The card should include a printed or handwritten *Congratulations!*

1

LANGUAGE FOCUS

You can use this language to congratulate someone formally:

| Please accept my congratulations | on | your promotion. |
| I would like to congratulate you I'm writing to | | receiving this year's sales award. |

You can congratulate more informally like this:

| Congratulations on | your graduation! the new arrival! |

Write sentences for the situations below. Use a different expression each time. Congratulate:

a   a co-worker on her promotion (informal)

_____

_____

b   a business acquaintance on the opening of his company's Milan branch (formal)

_____

_____

c   a co-worker on his twentieth year of employment with your company (formal)

_____

_____

2 Work with a partner. For the events below, would you send an email or greeting card?

1   a wedding
2   the opening of a new branch
3   a co-worker leaving the company
4   the birth of a child
5   a sales award

3 Match the sentences with the events in exercise 2.2.

a ☐ I wish you every success with the new venture.

b ☐ You worked very hard last year, and I am delighted your efforts have been rewarded.

c ☐ I would like to wish you both a long and happy life together.

d ☐ I am sure you will be very successful in your new position.

e ☐ Wonderful news! You must be thrilled!

3 A letter of congratulation

Circle the six correct alternative words, then write the corrected letter.

Dear Vernon,

I am ¹ *writing / write* to congratulate you ² *on / to* your appointment ³ *as / for* Vice President of GL Electronics.

I know that you ⁴ *will / have* achieve great success in your new job, and I look forward to continued ⁵ *co-operate / co-operation* between our two ⁶ *company / companies*.

Sincerely yours,

Miranda Finkelstein

Miranda Finkelstein

_____

_____

_____

_____

_____

_____

4 Writing task 1

Use the notes below to write a letter of congratulation to a business acquaintance. You can use the letter above as a model, and ideas from exercise 3.

- write to Rosa Santos
- she has won her company's Employee of the Year award
- you know that she has worked very hard
- you think she has a great future with the company

5 Expressing sympathy

TIP!

A short letter is more appropriate than an email for a sympathy or condolence letter. Writing it by hand makes it more personal.

LANGUAGE FOCUS

To express sympathy for an illness or accident, you can use:

| I was very | sorry to hear of | your | illness. |
| We were so | | | accident. |

For condolences, you can use:

| I was | (deeply) | shocked | to hear of | your husband's death. |
| We were | | saddened | | Matthew's passing. |

Use the sentence endings to complete the letter of sympathy to Mei (A) and letter of condolence to Sergei (B) below.

a   just concentrate on getting better.
b   if there is anything I can do to help.
c   my sincerest sympathy at this difficult time.
d   I hope you get well soon.

Dear Mei,

I was very sorry to hear about your accident, and _____
_____
_____

Don't worry about work for a while – _____
_____

We all look forward to welcoming you back to the office when you are ready.

With very best wishes,

Tom Nakamura

Dear Sergei,

I was deeply saddened to hear of the death of your mother. Please accept _____
_____

Please let me know _____
_____
_____

Sincerely,

Elaine Border

6 Writing task 2

 Work with a partner. Write a letter of sympathy using the information below.

> You have just heard that your Korean client, Kim Soon Yong, is in the hospital. He has appendicitis. You hope to meet him during your visit to Seoul next month.

7 Thanking

1

USEFUL LANGUAGE

In most situations, you can use:

It was very kind of you to invite me to dinner				last Friday.
Thank you Thanks*	(very much) (so much)	for	inviting me to dinner the wonderful dinner	

*Usually used in less formal writing

Write sentences for the situations below.

a your hospitality last weekend

_____

_____

b the birthday card

_____

_____

c helping me set up my computer yesterday

_____

_____

d the thoughtful gift

_____

_____

2 Work with a partner. Write a similar sentence using your own ideas.

_____

_____

8 A thank-you email

TIP!

You can thank someone using email, or more personally, by writing a letter by hand. You can also send a thank-you card.

Read the email and fill in the blanks using the words below.

during   of   in   to   around   on   for   at

Delete   Reply   Reply All   Forward   Print

Dear Mr. Kahn,

I arrived home safely yesterday, and would like to thank you
1 _____ all your help 2 _____ my stay
in Karachi, and the delicious dinner 3 _____ my final
evening. The chicken tikka was wonderful.

My trip 4 _____ Pakistan was very useful, and I look
forward to meeting you again 5 _____ the annual
sales meeting 6 _____ Paris next year. I will be able to
show you 7 _____ the city and return your hospitality.

I have attached a few photographs 8 _____ the
dinner.

Thank you again.

Sincerely yours,

Veronique LaCroix

9 Writing task 3

Write a thank-you letter to a business acquaintance. Use your own ideas or the notes below. You can use the letter above as a model.

— Write to Ms. Quinn.
— You visited Dublin, Ireland.
— You arrived home on Monday.
— Thank her for looking after you and the enjoyable time at the pub on your last evening.
— The music was excellent.
— The trip to Ireland was extremely valuable.
— You look forward to meeting her again next year in your city / country.

Review 3

1 Interoffice memos

1 Read the two memos.

A

Tech-loc Corp

MEMO

DATE: October 31

TO: Data Storage Dept, Cabel Building

FROM: Jack Lee, Head of Office Services

SUBJECT: ....

Your office reorganization will take place November 11–12. Please empty all cupboards and shelves and pack your belongings by noon on Friday, November 10. You are advised to take personal items home with you. The I.T. Department will be responsible for computers, printers, etc.

The building will be closed from 1:00 p.m. Friday until 8:00 a.m. Monday morning. Staff cannot enter the building during the weekend.

If you need more packing cases, please contact Spencer Fu. Thank you for your co-operation during this time.

B

From:	helen.scott@tech-loc.com
To:	Data storage team
Cc:	
Subject:	....

We are pleased to inform you that a meeting has been arranged to explain the new data storage system on Wednesday, November 8. We are very fortunate that Yoko Kawamoto, who designed the system, is available to present the design and answer questions.

Ms. Kawamoto will be taken on a tour of the Data Storage Department at 10:00 a.m. The meeting will be held in the Main Conference Room of the Cabel Building at 11:00 a.m. A buffet lunch will be served at 1:00 p.m.

All members of the data storage team are requested to attend the meeting.

Many thanks,

Helen Scott

2 Write in a suitable subject line for each memo.

3 Find words and phrases in the memos that have the same or similar meanings as the ones below.

a it's a good idea if you … _____
b get in touch with _____
c help _____
d tell _____
e lucky _____
f asked _____

How are the words and phrases on the right different from those on the left?

4 Write the questions about the memos.

a When _____?
   November 11–12.
b Who _____?
   The I.T. Department.
c Can _____?
   No, they can't.
d Where _____?
   In the Main Conference Room of the Cabel Building.
e What _____?
   She will explain the design of the new storage system.

2 Social situations

1 Match the situations (a–d) with the messages (1–4) below.

a thanks ☐
b congratulations ☐
c sympathy ☐
d seasonal greeting ☐

1

We're sorry
to hear about
your illness.
Get well soon!

2

I had a great time at
the barbecue. It was
very kind of you to
invite me.

4

Good luck in
your new
position. I'm
sure you'll be
a great
success.

3

I wish you and your team a happy new
year. I look forward to working with
you in the future.

2 Now write your own short messages for the situations below. Write at least two sentences for each one. You can use formal, neutral, or informal language.

a Congratulate a co-worker on completing her M.B.A.

_____

_____

b Thank a business acquaintance in the U.S. for inviting you to dinner.

_____

_____

c Express sympathy with a business acquaintance who has had an accident.

_____

_____

d Congratulate a business acquaintance on the opening of a new branch office.

_____

_____

e Express your condolences to the colleagues of a business acquaintance who has died.

_____

_____

f Thank a business acquaintance in China for helping you on a recent business trip to Beijing.

_____

_____

3 Pairwork dictation

1 Work with a partner. Take turns reading sentences to your partner, who will write them down.
Student A: Use the sentences on page 109.
Student B: Use the sentences on page 110.

> **LANGUAGE FOCUS**
>
> Could you say that again?
> Could you speak more slowly?
> How do you spell "_____"?
> What's the (fourth) word?

Now write the sentences that your partner reads out to you.

a _____

b _____

c _____

d _____

e _____

f _____

2 When you have finished, compare your sentences with your partner's page. Did you spell everything correctly?

---

4 Discussing proposals

1 Read the proposal below.

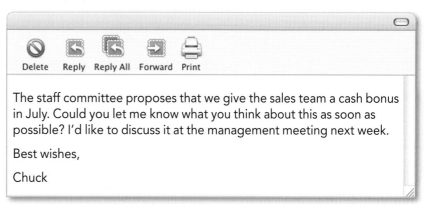

The staff committee proposes that we give the sales team a cash bonus in July. Could you let me know what you think about this as soon as possible? I'd like to discuss it at the management meeting next week.

Best wishes,

Chuck

2 Read the responses to the proposal and label them: "A" (agree), "D" (disagree), or "U" (uncertain).

a To be honest, I don't like that idea. The costs would be very high. ☐

b I think that's a great idea. For one thing, it would improve staff
   morale after the cutbacks last month. ☐

c I'm not sure about that. Can I get back to you? I'd like to consult
   the supervisors on my team. ☐

d I'm in favor of the proposal. The sales team worked hard to
   improve sales this year. ☐

e That sounds interesting but can I think about it? It may not be a
   good idea. Employees on other teams wouldn't be happy about it. ☐

3 Now write your own responses to the proposal below.

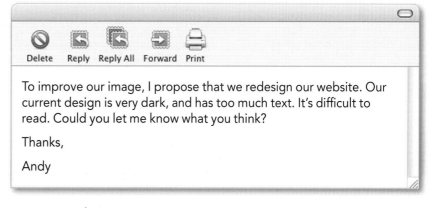

To improve our image, I propose that we redesign our website. Our current design is very dark, and has too much text. It's difficult to read. Could you let me know what you think?

Thanks,

Andy

a agree and give a reason

_____

b disagree and give a reason

_____

c express uncertainty and give a reason

_____

5 Correct the mistakes

Below is the first draft of a short report sent by email. There are two mistakes in each of the following:

— spelling
— punctuation
— capitalization
— verb tenses
— prepositions

Find the 10 mistakes and correct them.

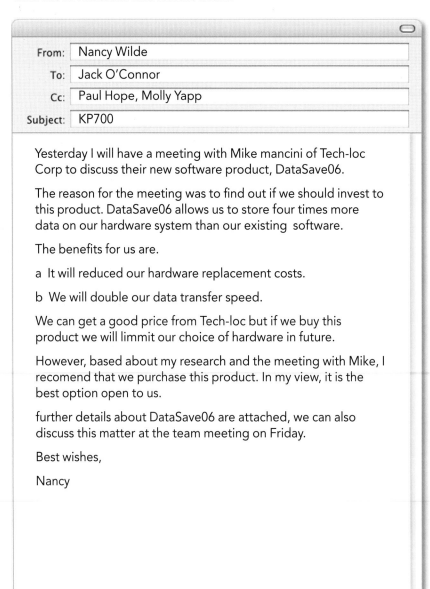

From:	Nancy Wilde
To:	Jack O'Connor
Cc:	Paul Hope, Molly Yapp
Subject:	KP700

Yesterday I will have a meeting with Mike mancini of Tech-loc Corp to discuss their new software product, DataSave06.

The reason for the meeting was to find out if we should invest to this product. DataSave06 allows us to store four times more data on our hardware system than our existing software.

The benefits for us are.

a It will reduced our hardware replacement costs.

b We will double our data transfer speed.

We can get a good price from Tech-loc but if we buy this product we will limmit our choice of hardware in future.

However, based about my research and the meeting with Mike, I recomend that we purchase this product. In my view, it is the best option open to us.

further details about DataSave06 are attached, we can also discuss this matter at the team meeting on Friday.

Best wishes,

Nancy

Pairwork dictation

Student A

Review 1

Student A, read these sentences to your partner:

a   I look forward to meeting you in the near future.
b   If you have any questions, please let me know.
c   Would you like to join me for lunch?
d   I'm afraid I have an appointment on that day.
e   Can you recommend a good hotel?
f   It's not definite, but I'm probably visiting Japan in June.

Review 2

Student A, read these sentences to your partner:

a   We have an extensive sales network throughout Europe.
b   Would you please send us your current catalogue.
c   This is to inform you that we have received your order dated May 3.
d   We would like to confirm that we will get a 5% discount.
e   We have instructed our bank to make the transfer.
f   This is a reminder that payment of invoice number 411 is three months overdue.

Review 3

Student A, read these sentences to your partner:

a   According to the schedule, the report was due yesterday.
b   The new equipment will be installed next week.
c   Our customers are concerned about health and safety issues.
d   During the past two years, sales have remained constant.
e   In the first quarter, profits fell sharply.
f   Can I get back to you later today?

Pairwork dictation

Student B

Review 1

Student B, read these sentences to your partner:

a   I will make the necessary arrangements for your visit.
b   I wonder if we could meet sometime next week.
c   Do you have any suggestions for sightseeing?
d   Is Wednesday afternoon convenient for you?
e   How about meeting Tuesday morning at your office?
f   Thank you very much for your kind invitation to dinner.

Review 2

Student B, read these sentences to your partner:

a   We would like to know more about your services.
b   Our company is a well-known importer of plastic goods.
c   We regret that the model you requested is out of stock.
d   I am writing in reference to order number J429.
e   Please find enclosed a copy of the invoice for your reference.
f   If we do not receive payment within one week, we will take legal action.

Review 3

Student B, Read these sentences to your partner:

a   Please let me know if there is a problem with the completion date.
b   The monthly sales meeting has been postponed.
c   I suggest that we negotiate a discount.
d   Last month, production costs rose sharply.
e   Could you let me know what you think?
f   Please accept my congratulations on your promotion.

Reference section

Formats

Emails

1 Writing an email

When you write an email your computer will look something like this:

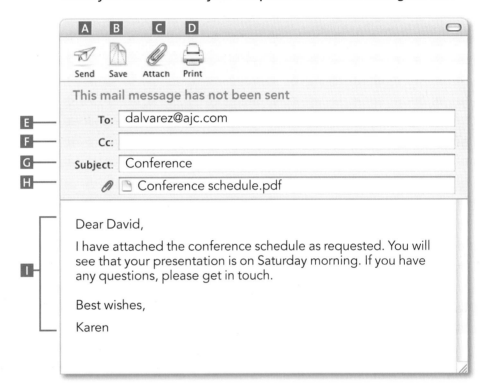

Click this when you want to …

a send your message.
b save your message.
c attach a document (text file, photographs, etc.).
d print your message.

This is where you …

e write the name of the person you are writing to.
f write the names of other people who will receive the same message.
g write what the message is about.
h see the title of a document (text file, photo, etc.) which is sent with the email message.
i write the body (main text) of the message.

Note: Cc = carbon copy   Bcc = blind carbon copy

2 Receiving an email

When you receive an email, your computer screen will look something like this:

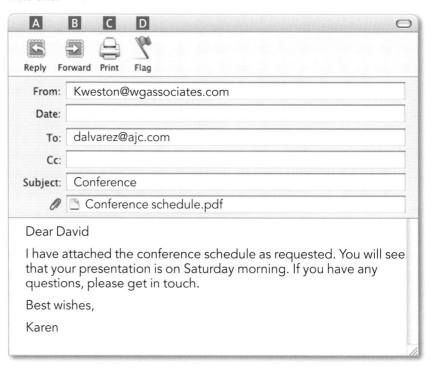

Click this when you want to …

a   reply to the message.
b   send the same message to another person.
c   print a copy of the message.
d   remember an important message.

Note: If the attachment is a graphic file, e.g. a map or photograph, it usually appears in the main text window. To open a text file attachment, click on the *Attachments* arrow, or the file icon.

3 Using the reply function

When you click the "reply" button, the body of your email might look like this:

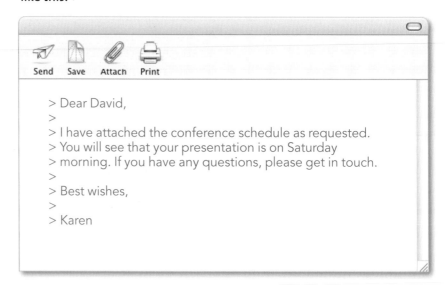

You can edit (change) the message you received, when you reply to someone. For example, David uses the main body of the email, but changes the salutation, complimentary close and signature:

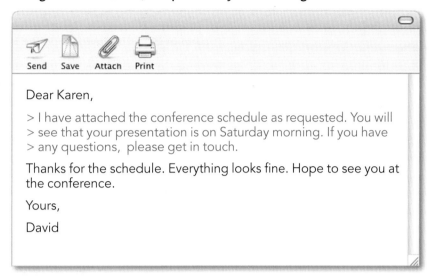

Dear Karen,

> I have attached the conference schedule as requested. You will
> see that your presentation is on Saturday morning. If you have
> any questions, please get in touch.

Thanks for the schedule. Everything looks fine. Hope to see you at the conference.

Yours,

David

Letters

1 The envelope

Your company may supply envelopes which include its name and address. If you are using a plain envelope, write your own name and address in the top left-hand corner:

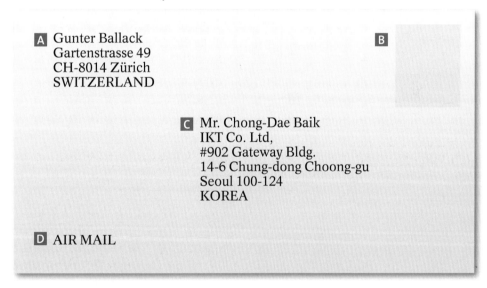

A Gunter Ballack
Gartenstrasse 49
CH-8014 Zürich
SWITZERLAND

B

C Mr. Chong-Dae Baik
IKT Co. Ltd,
#902 Gateway Bldg.
14-6 Chung-dong Choong-gu
Seoul 100-124
KOREA

D AIR MAIL

a Sender's full name and address. Write this clearly.
b Postage stamp(s).
c Full name and address of the person you are sending the letter to. Write this clearly. You can write all of this section in capital letters if you like.
d Special instructions*

*Some other special instructions:

CONFIDENTIAL
REGISTERED MAIL
SPECIAL DELIVERY
PRINTED MATTER
MEDIA

2 Writing a business letter

If you do not know the name of the person you are writing to, use *Dear Sir or Madam*. If you know the person's name, use *Dear Mr. / Ms. ...* . End with *Sincerely*, and sign yourself with your full name.

The simplest business letter format is the full-block format, with all the parts of the letter lined up on the left-hand side of the paper.

A — **ELLIS AUTOPARTS INC.**

1021 East 160th Street Bronx, NY 10443
phone: 718-561-2000
email: ellis@autoparts.com www.ellisautoparts.com

B —
Victor Duma
Sales Department
Colorado Autos Inc.
4610 Harrison Road
Denver, CO 80116

C — July 23, 2005

D — **Subject: Catalog**

E — Dear Mr. Duma,

F — Enclosed please find our latest catalog, which you requested during our phone conversation yesterday. You will see that it contains a number of interesting new items.

I look forward to hearing from you.

G — Sincerely,

H — *Barbara Windsor*

Barbara Windsor (Ms.)

a Letterhead: The name and address of your company. It would usually include email address, phone and fax numbers, and website address. If you are not using letterhead paper, write your company name and contact details at the top of the page on the right.

b Inside address: The full name and address of the person you are writing to.

c Date: Write this on the left, under the address of the person you are writing to. Leave a space between their address and the date.

d Subject line: This is optional (you don't have to use it).

e	Saluation:	Use the person's title (Mr., Ms., Dr., etc.) and a colon or comma at the end. A colon is more formal.
f	Body:	Start a new paragraph for each topic. You can indent* the first line of each paragraph if you like.
g	Closing:	Position this on the left-hand side of the page. Start with a capital letter, and write a comma at the end.
h	Signature:	Write this by hand. Type your full name below your handwritten signature.

*Indent = leave five blank spaces at the beginning of a line (one tab on a word processor).

3 Writing a personal letter

A personal letter to a business acquaintance can be written by hand or on a computer. If you are not using letterhead writing paper, write your address and the date on the right. You do not need to write the address of the person you are writing to.

a Heading: Your address. This is not necessary if you use letterhead

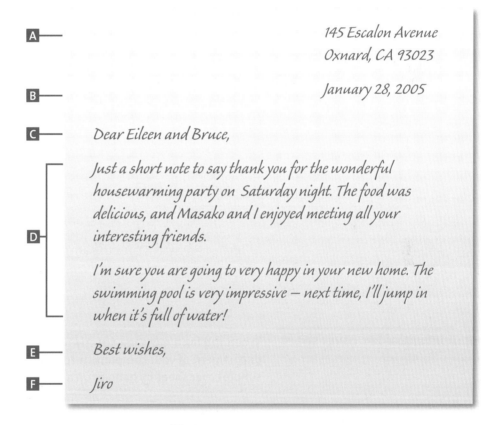

A

> 145 Escalon Avenue
> Oxnard, CA 93023
>
> January 28, 2005

B

C — Dear Eileen and Bruce,

D —
> Just a short note to say thank you for the wonderful housewarming party on Saturday night. The food was delicious, and Masako and I enjoyed meeting all your interesting friends.
>
> I'm sure you are going to very happy in your new home. The swimming pool is very impressive — next time, I'll jump in when it's full of water!

E — Best wishes,

F — Jiro

writing paper.

b	Date:	Write this on the right, under your address. Leave a space between your address and the date.
c	Salutation:	Capitalize the first word and the name, and use a comma at the end.
d	Body:	Start a new paragraph for each topic. You can indent the first line of each paragraph if you like.
e	Closing:	Position this on the left-hand side of the page. Start with a capital letter, and write a comma at the end.
f	Signature:	Your own name. Even if you write a personal letter on a computer, sign it by hand.

Fax cover sheets

1 A formal fax cover sheet

Always include a cover sheet when you send a fax to another company, or to someone you don't know well in your company. Your company may supply a customized fax cover sheet. If not, you can prepare your own and save it as a template:

SINGTEC LTD,
8 Park Boulevard, #27-04
Singapore 0369

Tel/Fax: +65-6312-2709
Email: jeffchang@aol.com

TO:	Lisa Mackenzie
FROM:	Jeff Chang
SUBJECT:	Instruction booklet
DATE:	June 2, 2005
No. OF PAGES:	6

Dear Ms. Mackenzie,

Following our telephone conversation this morning, I am sending you a fax copy of the instruction booklet for our XP3-200 digital voice recorder. I will mail you a printed copy of the booklet as soon as it becomes available.

Thank you for you interest in our products.

Sincerely,

Jeff Chang

Jeff Chang

Manager,
Customer Relations Department

2 A informal fax cover sheet

When you fax a message directly to someone you know well in another department of your company, or to a private address, you can write a simple cover sheet by hand or on a computer:

November 5, 2005

Miguel,

I saw this cartoon in the paper this morning. Thought you would enjoy it!

Best wishes,

Anita

Memos

*Note: "memo" is short for "memorandum" (Latin: "something to remember")

You can use memos* to communicate with people in your own company. Memos are suitable for reminders, announcements, and exchanging information. They can be written as emails or on paper.

Paper memos can be distributed by hand or posted on a notice board. If your company does not supply preprinted memo paper, be sure to include the headings in the example below. You do not need to write a salutation, but you should sign or initial the memo by hand.

A preprinted memo page may look like this:

MESA SPORTS SUPPLIES

MEMO

To: All employees
From: Vincent Ohly
Date: Jan 23, 2006

Following the successful launch of the computer training department last year, we now plan to offer a range of new computer courses to all employees. Please discuss your training requirements with your manager by June 1 and enroll for a course by June 10.

Vincent Ohly

Vincent Ohly
Personnel Manager

The same message received as an email memo may look like this:

From:	Vincent Ohly
Date:	January 23, 2006
To:	All employees*
Subject:	Computer courses

Following the successful launch of the computer training department last year, we now plan to offer a range of new computer courses to all employees. Please discuss your training requirements with your manager by June 1 and enroll for a course by June 10.

Vincent Ohly
Personnel Manager

*Use the "Group" setting in your email application to send a message to a number of people.

Reports

A report can be short and informal, similar in layout and style to an interoffice memo. It can be distributed as an email or an email attachment, with the subject / title, date, and the name of the writer at the top.

Longer reports are often more formal and can be presented as email attachments or on paper. The writer's name can be at the top of the page or at the end of the report.

Always try to present your information as clearly as possible. Pay attention to layout and include:
— a subject / title
— an introduction
— the body of the report
— a conclusion (with recommendations, if necessary).

Here is a short report in the form of an email attachment.

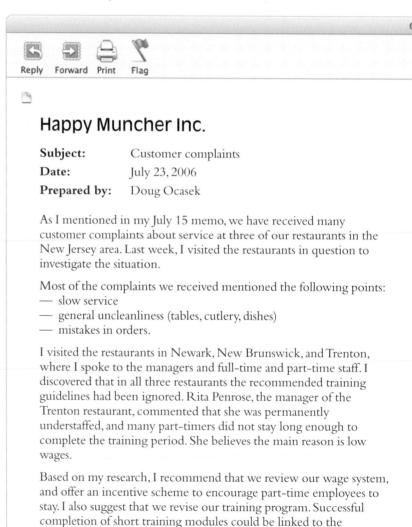

Happy Muncher Inc.

Subject: Customer complaints
Date: July 23, 2006
Prepared by: Doug Ocasek

As I mentioned in my July 15 memo, we have received many customer complaints about service at three of our restaurants in the New Jersey area. Last week, I visited the restaurants in question to investigate the situation.

Most of the complaints we received mentioned the following points:
— slow service
— general uncleanliness (tables, cutlery, dishes)
— mistakes in orders.

I visited the restaurants in Newark, New Brunswick, and Trenton, where I spoke to the managers and full-time and part-time staff. I discovered that in all three restaurants the recommended training guidelines had been ignored. Rita Penrose, the manager of the Trenton restaurant, commented that she was permanently understaffed, and many part-timers did not stay long enough to complete the training period. She believes the main reason is low wages.

Based on my research, I recommend that we review our wage system, and offer an incentive scheme to encourage part-time employees to stay. I also suggest that we revise our training program. Successful completion of short training modules could be linked to the incentive scheme mentioned above.

I look forward to receiving your comments on my recommendations.

Greeting cards and condolence cards

Greeting cards are often used for particular occasions. Here are some typical examples.

Christmas / New Year (to a business acquaintance – formal)

Note: Christians often send a card with the message "Merry Christmas and a Happy New Year". If the receiver is not a Christian or you are not sure about his or her religious beliefs, "Season's Greetings" or "Happy Holidays" is the most appropriate greeting.

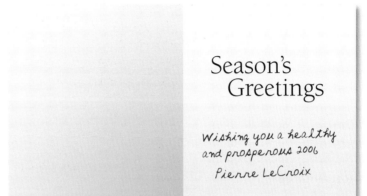

Season's Greetings

Wishing you a healthy and prosperous 2006
Pierre LeCroix

For the situations below, you can write a short letter or send a card. The inside of the card may be blank or have a pre-printed message.

Congratulations

We would like to wish you both a long and happy life together.
Very best wishes from Jiro and Yumiko Arakawa

Marriage
(to a co-worker – formal)

Birth
(to a co-worker – informal)

Congratulations

Wonderful news!
You must be thrilled!

Fond regards,
Rebecca

Thinking of You

Very sorry to hear about your accident.

Get well soon!
Than-Huong

Sympathy
(to a co-worker – formal)

We were very saddened to hear of your wife's passing. Please accept our deepest sympathy at this difficult time.

Sincerely,

Miroslav Wajda and everyone in the production department

Condolence
(to a business acquaintance – formal)

Thank you
(to a business acquaintance – informal)

Thanks so much for a wonderful party. Terrific food and great company!

See you soon,

Ron and Vera

Postcards

People often send postcards to their co-workers when they go on vacation. Messages are usually:
— short: three or four sentences
— informal, e.g. use of incomplete sentences
    Having a great time in … / Wish you were here.
— descriptive, e.g. use of adjectives
    wonderful, hot, relaxing, boring

Dear All,

Having a great vacation in Finland. The weather isn't so good, but the scenery is beautiful, and the people are really friendly. See you soon.

Best wishes,

Paul

Personnel Department
Western Electronics
Crown Building, Station Rd,
Croydon, Surrey, CR0 4BS
ENGLAND

Job résumés

Before you send off a job résumé, ask yourself these questions:
— Is it well-organized?
— Is it easy to read?
— Are there any spelling mistakes?

A MARC SIGNAC
505 Laval Street
East Montréal QC H4L 6N1
Canada

B EMPLOYMENT OBJECTIVES
Full-time position as marketing manager

EDUCATION
C 1998–2001   University of British Columbia, Vancouver
Bachelor of Science in Business Administration
D Major: Marketing
Related courses: History of advertising,
Multinational marketing, Marketing research

EMPLOYMENT EXPERIENCE
2003–present   VA Pharmaceuticals Inc., Chicago
Assistant Marketing Manager; coordinated
research into Canadian market
2001–2003   Ross Marketing Ltd., Montréal
Marketing assistant; created media kits and
participated in developing promotional campaigns

SKILLS   Proficient in all major software applications, e.g.
Microsoft Word, Excel, Power Point
French: fluent
Spanish: intermediate

INTERESTS   Cooking, Hang-gliding, Marathon running

REFERENCES   Available on request

a Write your full name, street address, telephone number(s), and email address.
b Write headings in capital letters, and start at the left margin.
c Write dates at the left margin. Put the most recent date at the top of each section.
d Set the information in each section one or two centimeters to the right, to allow space for dates.

The résumé is only about you, so you can shorten sentences like this:

I co-ordinated research …   — *Co-ordinated research …*
I created media kits …   — *Created media kits*
I am proficient in …   — *Proficient in …*

Section 2 Common features of written English

1 Salutations and closings

1 Business letter or email

*In a business letter or email salutation, you can use a comma (,) or a colon (:). A colon is more formal.

SALUTATION

If you know the person's name:

Dear + title + family name + colon or comma*	Dear Mr. Vronsky: Dear Ms. Berg: Dear Mr. Vronsky, Dear Ms. Berg,

If you don't know the person's name:

Dear + Sir or Madam: Dear + person's position: Dear + department's name: Dear + company name:	Dear Sir or Madam: Dear Personnel Manager: Dear Personnel Department: Dear Amazon:

CLOSING

Sincerely, Sincerely yours,	your handwritten signature (full name) + your typewritten name	Sincerely, *Jessica Wong* Jessica Wong

2 Formal social letter

SALUTATION

Dear + title + family name + comma	Dear Ms. Everett, Dear Prof. Evans, Dear Dr. Berg,

CLOSING

Sincerely, Sincerely yours	+ your handwritten signature (full name)	Sincerely, *Jessica Wong*

3 Informal letter

SALUTATION

Dear + given name,	Dear Setsuko,

CLOSING

Best wishes, Kind regards,	+ your signature (given name):	Best wishes, *Yuri* Kind regards, *Hideo*

4   Informal email

SALUTATION	
Dear + given name, Given name,	Dear Brad, Brad, Hi! (very informal)

Note: If you often write emails to someone you know well, you can omit a salutation.

CLOSING		
See you, Bye for now,	+ your given name:	See you, Linda Bye for now, Pedro

2 Beginnings and endings

1   Business letter or email

BEGINNING
(new subject) I am writing about … (reply) I am writing in response to your letter of January 22, 2006. Thank you for your email dated October 5, 2006.

ENDING
Thank you once again. I look forward to hearing from you.

2   Formal social letter or email

BEGINNING
(new subject) I am writing about (next week's trip). (reply) Thank you for your email dated March 10, 2006. I was very pleased to hear from you.

ENDING
I hope to meet you again in the near future. I look forward to hearing from you. Please give my regards to everyone.

3 Informal social letter or email

> **BEGINNING**
>
> (new subject)
> How are you?
> Hope you are doing well.*
> (reply)
> Thanks for your email.
> Good to hear from you.
>
> **ENDING**
>
> See you soon.
> Write soon!
> Take care.
> Regards to everyone!

*In informal writing, we can leave out the subject *I* in *I hope* …

Section 3 — Capital letters, punctuation, and spelling

1 Capital letters

Use capital letters (upper case):

— at the beginning of a sentence:
   People who work sitting down get paid more than people who work standing up.

— for names of people, schools, and companies:
   Akio Morita; Harvard Business School; Evergreen

— for brand names and products:
   Prada; Renault; Snickers

— for a person's title:
   Ms. Sontag; Dr. Strangelove; Prof. Park

— for some abbreviations:
   C.E.O. (Chief Executive Officer); M.B.A. (Master of Business Administration)

— for names of countries, places, and streets:
   Colombia; Trafalgar Square; Park Avenue

— for the main words in titles of movies, books, songs, and magazines:
   Psycho; Bonfire of the Vanities; The Girl from Ipanema; Business Week

— for days of the week, months of the year, and special days:
   Wednesday; July; Thanksgiving Day

Use only capital letters (block capitals) when you fill out forms by hand:

SERGIO PONTE
14 BIRDNEST PLACE
MILL VALLEY, CA 94922
U.S.A.

2 Punctuation

Punctuation makes your writing easier to understand. The most common punctuation marks are:

1 Period (.)
Use a period:
— at the end of a complete sentence, when this is a statement:
I'm leaving for Europe tomorrow.
— after an abbreviation:
Mr.; Ms.; Dr.; Prof. etc.
— in units of money:
$5.99 € 35.50
— in units of time (U.K.):
8.30 10.00
— in email and website addresses:
sjprice@hotmail.com www.oup.com

2 Comma (,)
A comma shows a short break in a complete sentence. Use it in a long sentence before a linking word like *but* or *so*:
I wanted to buy some milk, but the store was closed.
I was very tired, so I went straight to bed.

You can also use it in a list:
I want to visit France, Italy, and Germany.

Use a comma after the salutation in an informal letter or email:
Dear Ms. Perez,   Dear Andy,

Use a comma after the complimentary close in any letter or email:
Sincerely,   Sincerely yours,   Best wishes,   Bye for now,

3 Question mark (?)
Use a question mark at the end of a *yes/no* question, or a *wh*-question.
Are you free Monday morning?
What are you doing Monday morning?

4 Exclamation mark (!)
Exclamation marks are rarely used in formal business correspondence, but add expression (surprise, shock, pleasure) to informal writing, such as emails and postcards:
The beach is beautiful!
I saw Nicole Kidman at the airport!

5 Colon (:)
Use a colon before a list or quotation:
The convention center has excellent facilities: large and small meeting rooms, restaurants, and a gym.
He shouted: "Don't be late!"

And after the salutation in a formal business letter or email:
Dear Mr. Parkinson: Dear Sir or Madam:

6 Semicolon (;)
Use a semicolon to connect two clauses when the second clause gives extra information about the first:
I felt terrible after the flight; I had a headache and my legs hurt.
The meeting was very valuable; we learned a great deal about labor laws.

7 **Apostrophe** (')
In informal writing, use an apostrophe to show contractions:
That's a great idea.

Use an apostrophe to show possession:
Have you seen Sarah's laptop?
Mr. Kato's tickets haven't arrived yet.

If the word or name ends with an *s*, you can show possession in two ways:
Is this Ms. Holmes' desk?   *Is this Ms. Holmes's desk?*

8 **Quotation marks** (" ")
Use quotation marks before and after direct speech (the exact words someone says). Quotation marks contain the words and the punctuation (period, question mark, exclamation mark, etc.):
"It's on the table."
"Where's the police station?"

Do not use quotation marks in reported speech:
He said it was on the table.
She asked us to be quiet.

9 **Parentheses** ( )
Use parentheses to add extra information to a sentence. Notice that the sentence is still complete without the information in parentheses:
I met Mr. Callas the other day (he was here on business).
I would like to discuss our new accounts (especially the Ellis account), and decide how to proceed.

10 **Dash** (–)
In informal writing, you can use a dash in the same way as parentheses. If the additional information comes at the end of the sentence, use only one dash:
I met Mr. Callas the other day – he was here on business.
I would like to discuss our new accounts – especially the Ellis account – and decide how to proceed.

11 **Hyphen** (-)
A hyphen joins words in a compound word and numbers in a compound number: (a hyphen is shorter than a dash).
   mother-in-law   *medium-sized*
   thirty-five   *seventy-one*

3 Spelling

If you write on a computer, you probably use a spellchecker. If you don't have an English spellchecker, here is some useful advice on spelling.

1 **Common spelling mistakes**
People often spell these words incorrectly:

accommodation	*definitely*	*embarrassed*	*grammar*
misspell	*noticeable*	*receive*	*sandwiches*
separate			

People often make mistakes using these possessive forms:
Incorrect: *The building has it's own parking lot.*
Correct: *The building has its own parking lot.*

Incorrect: *They lost they're plane tickets.*
Correct: *They lost their plane tickets.*

Incorrect: *Is that you're dictionary?*
Correct: *Is that your dictionary?*

2 **Adjectives with final *l* and adverbs with *ll***
Always use one *l* at the end of an adjective:
hopeful   awful   careful

But use a double *l* in the adverb form:
hopefully   awfully   carefully

3 ***ie* and *ei***
When *ie* and *ei* have a long *ee* sound, you can use this rule:
i before e, except after c.
believe   chief   field   niece   piece

But when *ei* sounds like *ay*:
neighbor   weigh

After *c*, write *ei*:
ceiling   receive   receipt

4 **Plurals: words ending in *y***
If there is a vowel (*a, e, i, o, u*) before the *y*, add an *s* to make the plural:
boy – boys   day – days   key – keys

If there is a consonant (*b, c, d*, etc.) before the *y*, change the *y* to *i* and add *es.*
baby – babies   country – countries   memory – memories

5 **Verb forms: Simple present**
Don't forget to add *s* to the 3rd person singular (*he / she / it*) form:
eat – eats   read – reads   leave – leaves

With verbs ending in *y*, change the *y* to *ies*:
carry – carries   try – tries   fly – flies

There are some irregular verbs:
do – does   go – goes

6 **Verb forms: *ing***
With most verbs, add *-ing*:
eat – eating   read – reading   study – studying

With most verbs ending in *e*, drop the *e*:
have – having   hope – hoping   leave – leaving

With verbs ending in one *l*, just add *ing*:
feel – feeling   travel – traveling   sail – sailing

With verbs ending in *ie*, change *ie* to *y*:
die – dying   lie – lying

7 **Verb forms: Simple past tense**
With most regular verbs, add *ed*:
walk – walked   reach – reached   return – returned

With regular verbs ending in *e*, add *d* only:
save – saved   live – lived   phone – phoned

You must learn irregular verbs individually:
drive – drove   go – went   shine – shone

8 Compound nouns

Sometimes when we use two words together, the two words may become one word:

goodbye   businessman
email   wordprocessing

Section 4   General

1   Days, dates, and times

1   Days

Always use a capital letter at the beginning of a weekday:
Monday, Tuesday, Wednesday, etc.

In a list, you can use the first three letters (+ period) :

Mon.   *Arrive in Seoul*
Tue.   *Visit factory*
Wed.   *To Busan*

In a regular sentence, use the full word:
Are you free on Friday?
Looking forward to seeing you on Monday.

2   Months

Always use a capital letter at the beginning of a month:
August, September, October, etc.

In a list, you can use the short form (three letters + period):

Nov. 19   *On-site registration begins*
Nov. 20   *First day of conference*
Nov. 22   *Final day of conference*

3   Years

In a regular sentence you can use the full written form, but this is very unusual:
I think we first met in nineteen eighty-nine.

Use the full numeral form:
1998, 2001, 2008

You can use the short form (final two numerals) in plans and schedules:

To Production   Nov. 05
In Warehouse   Feb. 06

And in informal writing (with an apostrophe):
See you in '07!

4   Dates

At the beginning of a letter and in a regular sentence, write the date like this:
November 14, 2006
The Denver branch opened on May 6, 2005.

Use the numerical form* only on forms, for informal letters or emails, and in plans or schedules:
11/14/05
4/26/99

* In American English, the order is always month / day / year. In British English, the order is always day / month / year.

5 Times

In a regular sentence, you can write the hours like this:

Let's meet at   *six o'clock.*
                 6 o'clock.
                 6 p.m.
                 ~~*6 o'clock p.m.*~~

And the quarter and half hour times like this:

How about   *a quarter past six?*
             half past six?
             a quarter to seven?

But most writers use numerals only with a colon. You can add a.m. or p.m. if you like:

How about   *6:oo? / 6:00 p.m.?*
The train leaves at   *9:23 / 9:23 a.m.*

6 Prepositions

on + day: *Where should we meet on Friday?*
on + date: *We are leaving on July 24.*

           Note In American English you can omit *on* in informal writing:

           Where should we meet Friday?
           We're leaving July 24.

in + month: *I was in Australia in August.*
in + year: *She graduated in 2002.*
at + time: *See you at 7 o'clock.*

---

2 Numbers

In formal writing, spell out cardinal numbers (one, two, etc.) from 1 through 100:

Sixteen models are now available.
The company now has twenty-five branches in the E.U.

Use numerals for larger cardinal numbers:

We have 325 employees at the Chicago plant.
We employ 4,226 people worldwide.

Ordinal numbers (first, second, etc.) are used in the same way:

This is the third time we have ordered goods from you.
He finished the marathon in 220th position.

In lists and informal writing, you can use numerals for all numbers.

Note the positions of the commas in these numbers:

219   (no comma)
1, 219
41, 219
241, 219
3, 241, 219
33, 241, 219

---

3 Money and prices

In formal writing, write out smaller prices (under 100 dollars):

Membership is ten dollars.
We paid fifty dollars for the tickets.

Use numerals for larger prices, and place the dollar sign before the number:

My new computer cost $1,249.
Last month he earned $3,000.

Use numerals and a period for prices which include cents:

It cost $5.25.
The list price was $99.99.

In lists and informal writing, you can use numerals for all prices.

4 Currencies

* The euro is the currency of some countries in the E.U.

COUNTRY	CURRENCY	SYMBOL
Australia	Australian dollar	$
Brazil	real	R$
Canada	Canadian dollar	$
E.U. (European Union)	euro	€
Hong Kong	H.K. dollar	$
Indonesia	rupiah	Rp
Japan	yen	¥
Korea	won	W
New Zealand	N.Z. dollar	$
Thailand	baht	Bht / Bt
United Kingdom	pound	£
United States	U.S. dollar	$

5 Abbreviations

1 Length

cm.	centimeter(s)
m.	meter(s)
km.	kilometer(s)
in.	inch(es)
ft.	foot, feet
yd.	yard(s)
mi.	mile(s)

2 Time

a.m.	ante meridiem (before noon)	11 a.m.
p.m.	post meridiem (after noon)	6:30 p.m.
min., mins.	minute, minutes	
hr., hrs.	hour, hours	

3 Points of the compass

N., S., E., W.	north, south, east, west
NE., SW., etc.	northeast, southwest, etc.

4 Common abbreviations from Latin

e.g.	*exempli gratia* (for example)
etc.	*et cetera* (and more in the same way)
i.e.	*id est* (that is, in other words)
NB	*nota bene* (note well, take notice)
vs.	*versus* (against)

5 Personal titles

B.A.	Bachelor of Arts	*David Wang, B.A.*
B.S.	Bachelor of Science	*Veronica McTavish, B.S.*
M.A.	Master of Arts	*Keiko Takayama, M.A.*
Mr.	(man – married or single)	*Mr. William Davis*
Mrs.	(woman – married)	*Mrs. Deborah Davis*
Ms.*	(woman – married or single)	*Ms. Rosetta Garcia*
Ph.D.	Doctor of Philosophy	*John Smith Ph.D.*

* If marital status is unknown, use this.

6 Others

fwd.	forward
cc.	copy
re.	about, concerning
p., pp.	page, pages
No., no.	number

7 Some common symbols

#	number	*Ref. #3652*
@	at	*bcrumb@gol.com*
*	asterisk – to mark a note	*Price: $250 **
		*(*batteries not included)*
"	inch, inches	*6" × 4" photos*
'	foot, feet (twelve inches)	*The table is 5' long and 3' wide.*

8 Text-messaging

Text-messaging abbreviations like the ones below are mainly used only in informal messages to people you know well.

ABBREVIATION	DEFINITION	ABBREVIATION	DEFINITION
ATB	All the best	KIT	Keep in touch
ATM	At the moment	L8	Late
B4	Before	L8R	Later
B4N	Bye for now	NP	No problem
BTW	By the way	PLS	Please
C	See	R	Are
CU	See you	RU	Are you
CUL8R	See you later	SPK	Speak
DK	Don't know	SPK2 U L8R	Speak to you later
DUR	Do you remember?	THX	Thanks
EVRY1	Everyone	U	You
EZY	Easy	UOK	are you OK?
F2T	Free to talk	U2	You too
IC	I see	W8	Wait
IDK	I don't know	Y	Why?
JK	Just kidding	YR	Your

6 American English and British English differences

The most important differences are in spelling and vocabulary:

1 Spelling

The main differences in spelling are:

	AMERICAN ENGLISH	BRITISH ENGLISH
-or / *-our*	color, neighbor, favorite	colour, neighbour, favourite
-z- / *-s-*	organization, recognize	organisation, recognise *
-er / *-re*	theater, meter	theatre, metre
-l- / *-ll-*	canceled, labeled, traveler	cancelled, labelled, traveller

* Note: *z* is also used in British English.

2 Vocabulary

Some useful examples:

AMERICAN ENGLISH	BRITISH ENGLISH
apartment	flat
cellphone	mobile phone
(potato) chips	(potato) crisps
cookie	biscuit
drugstore	chemist
elevator	lift
first floor	ground floor
French fries	chips
gasoline, gas	petrol
one-way ticket	single (ticket)
parking lot	car park·
period (in punctuation)	full stop
sidewalk	pavement
subway (train)	underground, tube

3 Writing a business letter

	AMERICAN ENGLISH	BRITISH ENGLISH
Salutation	Dear Mr. Baker, OR (formal business letter) Dear Mr. Baker:	Dear Mr Baker (no period after Mr) (no comma after the name)
Closing	Sincerely, OR Sincerely yours,	Yours faithfully OR Yours sincerely (no comma)

7 Country and city names

In English, some country and city names are spelled (and pronounced) differently than the original language. Here are some examples:

COUNTRY NAME		CITY	
(original)	(English)	(original)	(English)
Belgique	Belgium	Antwerpen	Antwerp
Deutschland	Germany	München	Munich
		Köln	Cologne
Hellas	Greece	Athinai	Athens
Italia	Italy	Venezia	Venice
		Firenze	Florence
Österreich	Austria	Wien	Vienna
Polska	Poland	Warsawa	Warsaw
Suisse / Schweiz / Svizzera	Switzerland	Genève	Geneva

8 International street addresses

Here is a U.S. address:

Ms. Dorothea Lange
Intercommunications Inc.
1620 Bernard Street, Suite A
Huntington Beach, CA 92647
U.S.A.

The name of the state is usually written as two letters:

CA	California	CO	Colorado	CT	Connecticut
FL	Florida	MA	Maryland	TX	Texas

Here are some addresses in other countries:

Hong Kong:
Mr. Stanley Wong
Ultra Export Co. Ltd.
16 Shelter Street
Causeway Bay
HONG KONG

Thailand:
Mr. Prakit Posayakri
S&K Apparel Co. Ltd.
514 Vibhavadi-Rangsit Rd.
Chatuchak
Bangkok 10920
THAILAND

United Kingdom:
Ms. Laura Murray
Star Publishing Ltd.
22 Bristow Gardens
LONDON W8 8PD
U.K.

Japan:
Mr. Juichiro Yagi
Excel Publishing Co. Ltd.
Edomizaka Mori Bldg 6F
4-1-40 Toranomon
Minato-ku
Tokyo 105-8529
JAPAN

Germany:
Herrn Bernhard Vogts
AMZ GmbH
Haldenweg 6
Weilheim 72891
Germany

9 Internet addresses (URLs)

An Internet address or URL usually looks like this:
http://www.apple.com
http://www.bbc.co.uk
http://www.elt@oupjapan.co.jp

The last part of the address is called the *domain*, and can tell us something about the website.

Some important U.S. domains are:

These three domains can now be used by anybody.

.com*	Commercial (companies and for-profit websites)
.org*	Non-profit organizations
.net*	Network access groups (e.g. Internet service providers)
.gov	Federal governmental agencies
.edu	Educational institutions granting 4-year degrees (often .ac in other countries)
.mil	Military agencies and organizations

There are also 2-digit country domains. If there is no country code, the organization is probably based in the United States. Some examples of country domains are:

.au	Australia
.br	Brazil
.ca	Canada
.cn	China
.dk	Denmark
.de	Germany
.fr	France
.id	Indonesia
.jp	Japan
.kr	Korea
.kw	Kuwait
.mx	Mexico
.nz	New Zealand
.sg	Singapore
.ch	Switzerland
.uk	United Kingdom

OXFORD
UNIVERSITY PRESS

Great Clarendon Street, Oxford OX2 6DP

Oxford University Press is a department of the University of Oxford.
It furthers the University's objective of excellence in research, scholarship,
and education by publishing worldwide in

Oxford New York

Auckland Cape Town Dar es Salaam Hong Kong Karachi
Kuala Lumpur Madrid Melbourne Mexico City Nairobi
New Delhi Shanghai Taipei Toronto

With offices in

Argentina Austria Brazil Chile Czech Republic France Greece
Guatemala Hungary Italy Japan Poland Portugal Singapore
South Korea Switzerland Thailand Turkey Ukraine Vietnam

OXFORD and OXFORD ENGLISH are registered trade marks of
Oxford University Press in the UK and in certain other countries

ISBN-13: 978 0 19 453817 6
ISBN-10: 0 19 453817 6

Printed in China

ACKNOWLEDGEMENTS

*The publisher would like to thank the following for their permission to reproduce
photoraphs and other copyright material*: Alamy Images pp 7 (businesswoman/
ImageState), 23 (sign/David Crausby), 26 (restaurant/VIEW Pictures Ltd),
41 (Starbucks/Kader Meguedad), 41 (Microsoft/Chris Ivin), 43 (Avis/allOver
Photography), 61 (office worker/ImageState), 87 (conference call/Ace Stock
Ltd), 97 (forest worker/Index Stock); Corbis pp 23 (Times Square/Alan Schein
Photography), 26 (Harley-Davidson sign/Reuters), 26 (Sydney Opera House/W.
Perry Conway), 41 (Hyundai/Kim Kyun-Hoon), 43 (Epson OLED/Issei Kato/
Reuters), 99 (baby/Walter Hodges), 99 (businessman/Gabe Palmer); Getty Images
pp 99 (cutting ribbon/Britt Erlanson/The Image Bank), 102 (celebration/Rob
Brimson/Taxi); National Geographic Image Collection p 94 (Chicago/Mark
Segal); OUP pp 18 (Hong Kong/Photodisc), 23 (golf, restaurant/Photodisc),
100 (woman/Photodisc); PunchStock pp 9 (pen/image100), 99 (wedding/Brand
X Pictures), 99 (presentation/Digital Vision), 102 (barbecue/Design Pics),
102 (home office/Brand X Pictures), 102 (office birthday/Stockbyte); Rex
Features p 26 (Savoy hotel/Alex Segre).

Cover photography by: Shireen Nathoo Design and PunchStock
(meeting/Bananastock), (Asian businesswoman/Brand X Pictures), (making
notes/Bananastock), (Asian women/Digital Vision).

Illustrations by: Adrian Barclay pp 21, 77, 79, 85, 103; Mark Duffin pp 30, 46,
51, 53, 57, 82; Nigel Paige pp 12, 24, 40, 55, 67, 69, 88